A Treasury of
Critical Thinking Activities
PRIMARY

Contributors:

Roslind Curtis
Maiya Edwards
Fay Holbert

Editor-in-Chief
Sharon Coan, M.S. Ed.

Art Director
CJae Froshay

Product Manager
Phil Garcia

Imaging
Alfred Lau

Cover Design
Lesley Palmer

Publishers

Rachelle Cracchiolo, M.S. Ed.

Mary Dupuy Smith, M.S. Ed.

Blake Staff

Edited by Kate Robinson

Original cover and internal illustrations by Greg Anderson-Clift

Original internals designed and typeset by Precision Typesetting Services

This edition published by

Teacher Created Materials, Inc.
6421 Industry Way
Westminster, CA 92683
www.teachercreated.com
©2001 Teacher Created Materials, Inc.
Made in U.S.A.
ISBN-0-7439-3617-5

with permission from
Blake Education
Locked Bag 2022
Glebe NSW 2037

Contents

Introduction

Today, teachers face many challenges. One of these is teaching critical thinking skills in the classroom. The teaching and management strategies in this Book cater to all students but provide built-in opportunities for bright students. These strategies allow students to actively participate in their own learning. Blackline masters and task cards are ready to use and can easily be added to your existing teaching program.

How This Book Is Structured

Management Strategies

This section describes the key management strategies. Each management strategy is given a symbol which appears on the task cards and blackline masters throughout the book. In this section you'll also find helpful generic blackline masters to support these management strategies.

Teaching Strategies

Seven teaching strategies are targeted:

- Bloom's Taxonomy
- Creative Thinking
- Research Skills
- Questioning Skills and Brainstorming
- Renzulli's Enrichment Triad
- Thinking Caps
- Gardner's Multiple Intelligences

Each of these strategies has its own section:

Notes These provide an overview of the methodology of the teaching strategy and its practical application in the classroom.

Activities These include a wide range of teaching activities covering the main curriculum areas. They can be undertaken exclusively or in conjunction with activities from the other teaching strategy sections. They could also prompt you to develop your own activities.

Task Cards and Blackline Masters The activities are supported by a variety of ready-to-use blackline masters and task cards. Suggested management strategies are indicated by symbols in the top right-hand corner.

Management Strategies

by Maiya Edwards

Key Educational Qualities in the Management Strategies for Bright Students

Although the activities in this book are appropriate for all students, they particularly meet the needs of bright students. Linda Silverman, the Director of the Gifted Development Center in Denver, suggests that there are several approaches which work well when dealing with bright students in the classroom.

Find out what they know before you teach them.

This will prevent re-teaching what a student already knows.

Omit drills from their lives.

Bright students often learn and retain a concept the first time it is presented to them. Use drill only for the students who need it.

Pace instruction at the rate of the learner.

As bright students learn quickly, allow them to progress at their own rate.

Use discovery learning techniques.

Inductive learning strategies (such as those explained in the Bloom's Taxonomy model) are welcomed by these students.

Focus on abstract ideas.

Bright students enjoy the challenge of abstract concepts.

Allow them to arrive at answers in their own way.

Bright students enjoy devising their own problem-solving techniques.

Allow students to form their own cooperative learning groups.

Avoid always making the brightest student in the group responsible for the whole group's learning. Allow students to sometimes choose their own groups and work with other bright, motivated students.

Design an individual education plan.

This will cater to different learning rates.

Teach them the art of argument.

Since bright students have a tendency to argue anyway, teach them to understand when it is appropriate to argue and also to understand the reaction of others to their argumentativeness.

Allow students to observe.

Provide bright students with opportunities to observe without demanding immediate answers.

Be flexible in designing programs.

Provide the students with a variety of program alternatives, such as independent study, special classes, mentoring, and enrichment activities.

As many bright students are unable to achieve their full potential in the regular classroom, they can often become frustrated and begin to exhibit disruptive or aggressive behavior. Others withdraw from class activities or deliberately mask their abilities.

Providing activities for the entire class does not mean that the activities need to limit bright students or make them conform. We have devised a range of management strategies for the classroom which allow for the implementation of all the key educational qualities referred to above. Each strategy is practical, flexible, and easy to implement.

As you will see on the next few pages, we have given each strategy an easily recognizable symbol so that when these strategies are applied to the task card and blackline master activities, you will know immediately how to organize your classroom.

Management Strategies for the Mainstream Classroom

MANAGEMENT STRATEGIES

MAINSTREAM CLASSROOM

A range of classroom management strategies could be employed to promote and encourage the development of the talent of the students in your class. Any of the strategies listed below would help to achieve a positive classroom environment.

Management Strategies Suitable for the Mainstream Classroom

▼   Enrichment and Extension Activities

→   Learning/Interest Centers

●   Contracts

❖   Independent Research

■   Parent Involvement

✖   Peer Tutoring

✳   Competitions and Awards

◗   Mentoring

✴   Team Teaching

✦   Withdrawal Program

⊃   Mixed Ability Grouping

✚   Cluster Grouping

⇒   Vertical Grouping

♣   Field Trips

Below is a sample page from the sections that follow. The symbols relating to the classroom strategies are on the top of each Blackline Master (BLM) or Task Card.

These symbols indicate the best strategies to use.

The learning area utilized for the activity is found here.

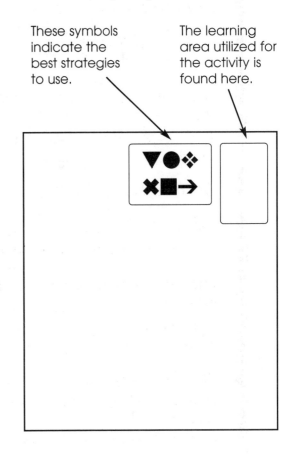

Management Strategies for the Mainstream Classroom

1 ▼ Enrichment and Extension Activities

These can be provided in all subject areas in a variety of ways:

- through task cards or blackline masters for higher level thinking skills
- research tasks
- special "challenge" days
- independent projects
- parent or mentor involvement

See BLM 4

2 → Learning/Interest Centers

These can be established in a corner of the classroom and designed to generate interest in a particular topic. They can:

- concentrate on one specific aspect of work being studied, such as "Weather Patterns"
- accommodate a special interest such as "Dinosaurs"
- extend certain skills such as advanced language/mathematical skills or thinking skills

See BLMs 4,5,6

3 ● Contracts

Students can be given a range of activities to complete which are set out around the room. Each student is given a list of the activities and asked to mark off each one as it is completed. The flexibility of this contract system appeals to the more capable student.

Contracts also have the advantage of being either teacher initiated or student initiated.

The teacher can set defined, targeted tasks or can allow the students to pursue their own interests with some guidance. There is also flexibility in the time allowed for the contracts. A contract can be extended over many weeks or set as a one session task.

See BLMs 1,2,3,4,7

4 ❖ Independent Research

Independent research provides an opportunity either within the school day or over a longer period to develop personal competencies through individual experiences. It may also involve interaction with others when designated. The research topic can be teacher initiated or student initiated.

It allows the students to launch in-depth investigations into something that they want to find out more about without constant supervision. It also encourages the students to use self-initiative and to employ their own style of learning to produce results.

The teacher's role changes from being the source of all knowledge to that of a facilitator and consultant.

See BLMs 1,2,3,4,7

5 ■ Parent Involvement

Establishing and maintaining a register of parents' interests, abilities, and availability can be invaluable when planning a program for the students in a classroom. Parents can be used to supervise cluster groups or extension activities and to encourage the exploration of individual interest areas. Some of the ways that parents could be kept abreast of classroom activities are via newsletters, resource packs, and information evenings.

Management Strategies for the Mainstream Classroom

6 ✖ Peer Tutoring

The more capable students can be paired with underachievers for some activities. This can be mutually beneficial for both students. The brighter students must develop an ability to clearly communicate an understanding of a topic or problem, while the underachiever receives the benefit of one-to-one coaching.

Outside the mainstream classroom, you can pair more able senior students with bright younger students. For example, pairing grade 5 or 6 students with grade 1 students works particularly well. The students could be paired for 30 to 60 minutes per week for activities such as writing, computers, art, or thinking games.

7 ✳ Competitions and Awards

Competition and award programs such as "Young Innovator of the Year" and "Tournament of the Minds" offer enrichment opportunities for all students, but particularly the brighter students. Students within the mainstream classroom could be provided with activities to prepare them for these tournaments and competitions.

Intra-class competitions and awards are a dynamic means of extending the entire class. There is a wide range of options:
- 30-minute quiz challenges
- knock-out quiz challenges throughout the term or year
- award schemes for independent research tasks (bronze award for a written and pictorial presentation; silver if something extra is included, such as a model, video, or Web page; and gold if the project is outstanding.)
- individual point scoring for tasks throughout the year. This scheme works well for all students in the mainstream classroom as points can be awarded for both outstanding work, additional work, or for improvement, effort, and positive attitudes, or for helping others. Points can be exchanged for play money at the end of each term. Students can bid at a class auction for donated items such as books, passes, toys, or for privileges such as extra computer time.

8 ◗ Mentoring

These programs link individual students with community members who have expertise in certain areas. Teachers can establish their own database of suitable people or seek the assistance of their district gifted and talented network to provide them with a list of mentors. Mentors can also talk to the class about specific interest areas and participate in some follow-up activities. This is a very productive way to inspire excellence and encourage independent interests.

9 ✶ Team Teaching

Students with various interests and talents meet with different teachers who specialize in specific subject matters. An excellent way to implement this is for three teachers to nominate three different fields of interest. The students then select which area of interest to pursue. This can be scheduled into the standard teaching week and run for two or three lessons, with a suitable assessment at its conclusion.

10 ✦ Withdrawal Program

Very exceptional students (or "gifted" students) can be withdrawn from a mixed-ability class for instruction with other more advanced students. This instruction can be provided by a specially appointed teacher, tutor, or a volunteer.

Management Strategies for the Mainstream Classroom

11 ⊃ Mixed Ability Grouping

When working on class assignments the students are placed in heterogenous groups (that is, groups with a range of abilities). The more able students assume the leadership roles with the others taking the tasks of writing and reporting. Roles can also be interchangeable or they can be rotated so that an even amount of work is done for all aspects of a task. An ideal size for mixed-ability groupings is three to five students.

See BLM 4

12 ✦ Cluster Grouping

All students can be clustered according to their relative ability in the classroom. Higher ability students can occasionally be clustered for full-time instruction within a mixed ability classroom. This works well when compacting a curriculum for the brighter students so that they are able to progress at their own rate.

See BLM 9

13 ⇛ Vertical Grouping

In classrooms which already contain several year levels, bright students of different ages can be combined with others who have similar interests, abilities, and aptitudes.

See BLM 4

14 ♣ Field Trips

This involves off-campus excursions to meet with experts in various fields, for example, museum experts, marine biologists, geologists. Field trips can provide an excellent basis for both cluster ability projects or independent research projects.

Self-Evaluation

It should be remembered that self-evaluation is a very powerful form of evaluation and should be an essential component of every classroom evaluation process.

This has been incorporated into the blackline masters on the following pages.

Blackline Masters

A range of blackline masters (BLMs) has been provided which can be used to assess and encourage students when using the above management strategies.

They are not activities in themselves but are designed to support the various teaching strategies presented in the book.

Teacher Records

For your own records, and so that you can show parents that you have given their children the opportunity to express the full range of skills, we have provided an individual record sheet suitable for each student, as well as a class record sheet.

See BLMs 7, 8

Name: _____

My Research Contract

Research Title: _____

Starting Date: _____ Completion Date: _____

Subject Area: _____

Brief Description: _____

Resources to be used: _____

Method of final presentation: _____

School time allocated to independent research: _____

Home time allocated to independent research: _____

Student's Signature: _____

Teacher's Signature: _____

Self-Evaluation:

The best thing about my independent research was: _____

_____

_____

The thing I found hardest to do was: _____

_____

_____

I could improve this by: _____

_____

_____

Teacher Comment

Name:

My Contract

My contract is to _____

I will start on _____ and finish by _____

✓ When finished	What I will do	How I feel about my work

Teacher Comment

Name:

My Research Checklist

Check (✔) the methods you have used for your independent research and hand this sheet in with your final presentation.

☐ Brainstorming

☐ Concept Mapping

☐ Library Research

☐ Interviewing

☐ Survey

☐ Questionnaire

☐ Experiment

☐ Graphs/Tables

☐ References Cited

☐ Have you provided an outline of your project?

Your final method of presentation can be very simple, or quite complex. Here are some suggestions. Circle the method you will use.

- Written Report
- Videotape
- Collection
- Letter
- Musical Composition

- Model
- Demonstration
- Scrapbook
- Play/TV Show
- Advertisement

- Comic Strip
- Magazine
- Computer Program
- Panel Discussion
- Invention

☐ Final Method of Presentation Chosen

☐ Final Presentation

☐ Own Evaluation of the Independent Study

☐ Teacher Evaluation of the Independent Study

Self-Evaluation

Name:

Checklist for Group Work

Other Group Members: _____

☐ I contributed new ideas. The best idea was _____

☐ I listened to the ideas of others. The best idea was _____

☐ I encouraged others in my group. This was by _____

☐ Something I could improve on is _____

_____

_____

Name:

Questionnaire for Learning Center or Enrichment Activities

Task: _____ Time taken: _____

How I did the activity and what I thought of it: _____

_____

_____

Future activities I would like included: _____

_____

_____

Name:

Learning Center Evaluation Sheet

ACTIVITY	DATE COMPLETED	EVALUATION (For example: too hard, too easy, boring, interesting)

Teacher Comment

Name:

Concept Mapping

Individual Record Sheet

Extension Procedures

Student Name: _____ Grade: _____

Students should complete at least one task or BLM from each extension procedure.

EXTENSION PROCEDURE	HOW MANY CARDS / BLMs COMPLETED?							
Bloom's Taxonomy (BT)	1	2	3	4	5	6	7	8
Creative Thinking (CT)	1	2	3	4	5	6	7	8
Research Skills (RS)	1	2	3	4	5	6	7	8
Questioning/Brainstorming (QB)	1	2	3	4	5	6	7	8
Renzulli's Enrichment Triad (RT)	1	2	3	4	5	6	7	8
Thinking Caps (TC)	1	2	3	4	5	6	7	8
Gardner's Multiple Intelligences (GI)	1	2	3	4	5	6	7	8

Teacher Comment

MANAGEMENT STRATEGIES

BLM 8

Class Record Sheet

Extension Procedures

Check that each student has completed at least one card
of BLM from each extension procedure.

STUDENT NAME	BT	CT	RS	QS	RT	TC	GI	COMMENT

Register of Parents' Interests

PARENT'S NAME	CHILD	CONTACT DETAILS	AVAILABILITY	AREA/S OF INTEREST

Bloom's Taxonomy

Notes and Activities

by Maiya Edwards

Overview for the Classroom Teacher

Bloom's Taxonomy

This model is one of the most frequently used extension procedures, for the development of higher level thinking skills. These skills are applicable to any subject and to any level of education, from pre-school to tertiary. Many varied teaching and learning activities can be developed using this as the basis.

The model enables all students to work through the process of developing a concept, with the more advanced students spending longer at the higher levels than the average student.

The thought processes involved in the different levels:

1. KNOWLEDGE — to recognize, list, name, read, absorb
2. COMPREHENSION — restate, describe, identify, review, explain
3. APPLICATION — apply, illustrate, connect, develop, use
4. ANALYSIS — interpret, categorize, contrast, compare, classify
5. SYNTHESIS — plan, create, invent, modify, revise
6. EVALUATION — judge, recommend, assess, criticize, justify

Average Student

1. Knowing and recalling specific facts

2. Understanding the meaning from given information

3. Using previously learned information in new situations

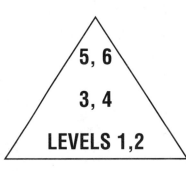

Talented Student

4. Breaking up the whole into parts

5. Putting together the parts to form a new whole

6. Making value judgements

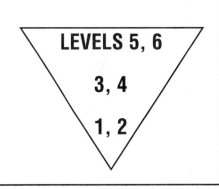

Overview for the
Classroom Teacher

From Convergent to Divergent Thinking

Use the actions in the boxes to achieve the outcomes in the arrows.

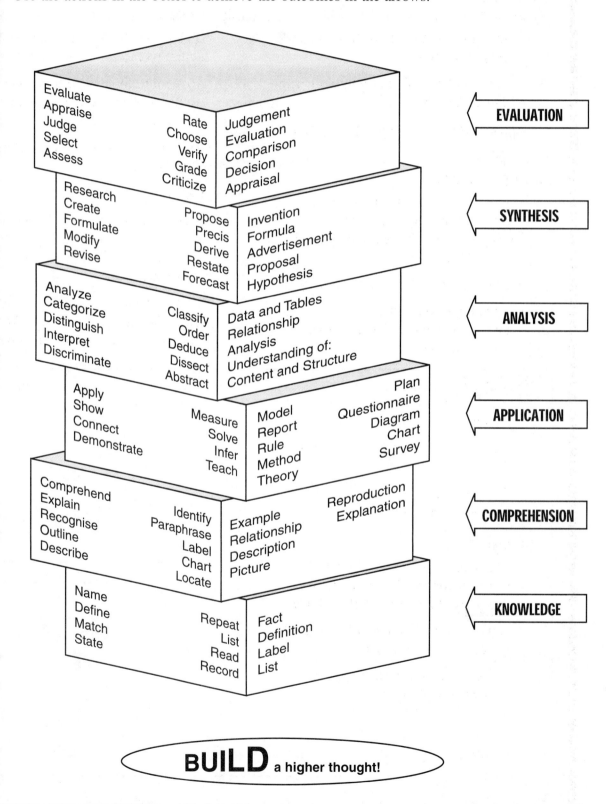

Evaluate
Appraise
Judge
Select
Assess

Rate
Choose
Verify
Grade
Criticize

Judgement
Evaluation
Comparison
Decision
Appraisal

EVALUATION

Research
Create
Formulate
Modify
Revise

Propose
Precis
Derive
Restate
Forecast

Invention
Formula
Advertisement
Proposal
Hypothesis

SYNTHESIS

Analyze
Categorize
Distinguish
Interpret
Discriminate

Classify
Order
Deduce
Dissect
Abstract

Data and Tables
Relationship
Analysis
Understanding of:
Content and Structure

ANALYSIS

Apply
Show
Connect
Demonstrate

Measure
Solve
Infer
Teach

Model
Report
Rule
Method
Theory

Plan
Questionnaire
Diagram
Chart
Survey

APPLICATION

Comprehend
Explain
Recognise
Outline
Describe

Identify
Paraphrase
Label
Chart
Locate

Example
Relationship
Description
Picture

Reproduction
Explanation

COMPREHENSION

Name
Define
Match
State

Repeat
List
Read
Record

Fact
Definition
Label
List

KNOWLEDGE

BUILD a higher thought!

Bloom's Taxonomy in English

Theme: Travel

Knowledge

- Ask students to list the different ways people can travel.

- Have students label different forms of transportation.

- Ask students to brainstorm different types of cars.

Comprehension

- Ask students to identify different forms of transportation from photographs. These can be placed around the room.

- Have students describe the family car.

- Encourage students to retell some facts they know about different forms of transportation.

Application

- Ask students to locate the nearest train station.

- Have them show the class the route they travel to school.

- Design a class mural showing all the different forms of transportation.

Analysis

- Ask students to categorize the different forms of travel under the headings of Air, Sea, Rail, and Road.

- Have students compare old forms of travel to modern forms.

- Make a class chart showing how students travel to school.

Synthesis

- Ask the class to predict how students will travel to school in the future.

- Challenge students to think what would happen if there were no more cars in the world.

- Have the students mime a different way to travel.

Evaluation

- Have students create little books showing their favorite ways to travel, for example, by train, car, or horseback.

- Ask students to calculate how long it takes them to get to school. Are there ways they could reduce this time?

- Have students choose the best way to travel from their home to a major sports venue in their city.

Name:

Travel

Knowledge

How many ways can you travel from one place to another?

List all the ways you know.

Application

Make a model of your family car.

Comprehension

Explain the main method you use to get home from school.

Name: _____

Travel

Synthesis
Invent a new way you could come to school.

Analysis
Survey the class to find out how many different ways they travel to school.

Number   Method

_____   _____
_____   _____
_____   _____
_____   _____
_____   _____
_____   _____
_____   _____

Evaluation
What changes would you recommend to road rules to prevent traffic accidents?

_____
_____
_____
_____
_____
_____
_____
_____
_____
_____
_____
_____
_____
_____
_____
_____
_____
_____
_____

Bloom's Taxonomy in Math

Knowledge

- Use number rhymes and fingerplays to teach concepts of counting and number facts.

  Examples:

  > **Number**
  > Ten little fingers
  > Ten little toes
  > Two little eyes and
  > One little nose.
  > One little mouth and
  > Why I declare!
  > Here are two little ears
  > Hiding under my hair.

  > **Subtraction**
  > Ten ships sailing,
  > sailing on the sea.
  > One sailed far away
  > and waved goodbye to me.

  > **Time**
  > My face is big
  > I tick all day
  > When my hands go round
  > What do I say?

Comprehension

- Have students find objects in the classroom to divide into the following categories: big and little, rough and smooth, square and round.

- Ask students to give examples of ways they could count to twenty. Suggest counting by ones, and then see if students can think of counting by twos, fives, tens, and so on.

Application

- Draw a picture such as the sun, a bell, or a box on the board and ask students to color exactly half the picture.

- Ask one student to teach another how to solve 10 – 4. Encourage them to use concrete objects to demonstrate. For example, put out ten pencils and take away four to show that there are six left.

Analysis

- Challenge students to find the relationship between 11 and 33.

- Ask them to classify all the objects in the learning center according to weight.

Synthesis

- Six times two equals 12. Challenge students to think of different formulas for arriving at the number 12.

- Have students plan a finger-puppet show to teach some number facts. Make a few suggestions about how they could decorate their fingers to represent different characters. Discuss ideas about what facts could be taught. They could use existing rhymes such as the ones mentioned under "Knowledge" as a basis for making up their own.

- Ask students to find a new way to measure the width of the classroom.

Evaluation

- Ask students to recommend the best way to work out how many different pets each student in the class has. For example, they could ask each student separately and add these up, ask the class to raise their hands, or prepare a simple questionnaire for each student to complete.

Bloom's Taxonomy in Math
Comprehension, Application, Analysis

Space

Draw the shadow of the tree.

Money

Cover each coin with the real one.
Circle the one that is worth the most.

Pattern

Complete the patterns.

Bloom's Taxonomy in Math

Analysis, Synthesis, Evaluation

Measurement

Write the days of the week in the correct order.

_____

_____

_____

Circle the day you like best. Circle the day you like least.

Number

Cross out three balloons.

Cross out five flowers.

8 take away 3 leaves _____

9 take away 5 leaves _____

Time

What takes the longest time to do?

Put these in the correct order (1 longest – 3 shortest):

☐ Brush your teeth   ☐ Blink Your eye   ☐ Walk to school

Bloom's Taxonomy for Health

Theme: Things We Do Every Day

Knowledge

- Ask students to tell you some of the things they do every day. Encourage ideas by suggesting we eat, we wash, we sleep.

Comprehension

- Have students cut out pictures from magazines which represent things they do every day.

- Ask them to draw pictures of things they do every day.

- Have them mime actions of what they do every day. Challenge the class to identify the actions.

Application

- Talk about things students do every day at school, such as reading. Ask them what they read and how they read.

- Suggest that students make a little book about themselves for the other students to read. Call it "My Favorite Things to do Every Day."

Analysis

- Read the story *Baby Gets Dressed* by Jane Cowley. This is a simple picture book which illustrates each step with two words and an action picture. Ask students,
  "What does Baby put on first?"

  "What does Baby put on next?"

  "How do you get dressed?"

- If this book is not available, ask students to analyze their own process of getting dressed each morning.

Synthesis

- Ask students to create their own books about what they eat every day by cutting photographs from a magazine and pasting them into a book. They can write their own captions underneath, such as "I eat cereal for breakfast."

- Provide old socks, buttons, and wool for students to make sock puppets. In groups of 4 to 5 have students make up a puppet show about a family eating breakfast. Suggest that some groups have their puppet family eating an unhealthy breakfast, while others are eating a healthy breakfast. (Link this with the "Evaluation" activity below.)

Evaluation

- Ask students which foods are healthy to eat and which are unhealthy. List them on the board and discuss reasons for their choices.

- Ask them to think about their own diets and decide whether or not they are eating food that is good for them.

Name: _____

Management Strategies:

Getting Dressed

Task: Write in each step as you dress yourself.

Then draw a picture of yourself fully dressed.

1   First, I _____

2   Next, I _____

3   Then I, _____

4   Then I, _____

5   Finally I, _____

Now I am dressed!

Name: _____

Eating

Warm-up Task: Which of these foods would you like to eat for lunch?

Answer **Yes** or **No**

1   A cheese sandwich   _____

2   A bucket of nails   _____

3   Leaves   _____

4   An apple   _____

5   Yogurt   _____

6   Snail sausages   _____

7   Grapes   _____

8   A chocolate worm   _____

9   A banana   _____

10 Spider jelly   _____

What to do: Imagine you can eat anything you want for breakfast.

List below and then draw a picture of what you would eat.

I would eat:

1 _____   2 _____   3 _____

Creative

Thinking

Notes and Activities

by Maiya Edwards

Overview of the Classroom Teacher

CREATIVE THINKING

NOTES

Creative Thinking Skills

In this section we are trying to move away from verbal and deductive skills and convergent thinking at factual levels; to encourage originality, inductive and inferential skills, and divergent thinking.

By recognizing and encouraging the potential of creative thinking in the classroom, the teacher can equip students with the open-ended, divergent thinking skills that are so useful in an ever-changing world.

Creativity can be developed in most students. This can be done by encouraging students to become independent thinkers who can modify, adapt, and improve the classroom environment. Teachers should encourage adventure and speculation by creating a positive atmosphere in which there is freedom to reflect, experiment, and take risks.

We can look at the creative process in five stages. Each of these stages involves the thinking skills and feelings which make up creativity.

Problem Awareness

This stage requires the ability to recognize that a problem exists, **sensitivity**, and **awareness**.

Incubation of Ideas

The third stage involves the production of intuitive and original possible answers before the facts have been checked out. Therefore, this synthesizing process of blending the old with the new requires fluency, flexibility, originality, elaboration, risk-taking, and imagination.

Illumination

The fourth stage requires the **awareness** necessary to provide an instant insight into the solution, often referred to as the "Aha!" moment.

Evaluation

The final stage requires the **perseverance** to evaluate the validity and full impact of the ideas generated.

Encouragement of creativity requires activities to challenge both thinking skills and emotional responses. This can be done by providing a supportive and stimulating classroom environment which will nurture these processes. On the following page are some ways in which the creative elements of thinking and emotional response can be enhanced.

Overview for the Classroom Teacher

Creativity Catalysts

Creativity catalysts can be used to generate innovative and original ideas.

Fluency

This initial stage combines the thinking skill of fluency with the emotional responses of imagination, curiosity, and originality to generate many different ideas, possibilities, and solutions.

Creativity catalysts:

- How many ways ...?
- List all the possible uses…
- Think of all the problems…
- Give as many ideas as you can…
- Add to this list…

Flexibility

This stage combines the thinking skill of flexibility with the emotional response of sensitivity to allow the students to blend the old with the new and to see things from many different points of view.

Creativity catalysts:

- What is the relationship between…?
- If you were…?
- Categorize…
- Rearrange…
- Substitute...

Originality

This stage combines the thinking skill of originality with the emotional responses of risk-taking and imagination. It encourages students to be inventive and use unique and unexpected approaches.

Creativity catalysts:

- Create…
- Design a different way to…
- How would you…?
- Invent…
- Predict…

Elaboration

This final stage combines the thinking skill of elaboration with the emotional responses of awareness and perseverance. It encourages students to expand, develop and add to ideas and materials.

Creativity catalysts:

- Add details to…
- Plan…
- Expand…
- Combine…
- Decide…

For more useful classroom catalysts, use the mnemonic **CREATIVITY** to generate further extension activities.

C	Combine, integrate, merge, fuse, brew, synthesize, amalgamate
R	Reverse, transpose, invert, transfer, exchange, return, contradict
E	Enlarge, magnify, expand, multiply, exaggerate, spread, repeat
A	Adapt, suit, conform, modify, alter, emulate, copy, reconcile
T	Thin out, minimize, streamline, shrink, squeeze, eliminate, understate
I	Instead of, substitute, swap, replace, exchange, alternate, supplant
V	Viewpoint change, other eyes, other directions, more optimistically, more pessimistically
I	In another sequence, rotate, rearrange, by-pass, vary, submerge, reschedule
T	To other uses, change, modify, rework, other values and locations
Y	Yes! affirm, agree, endorse, concur, approve, consent, ratify, corroborate

Creative Thinking in English

Theme: Circus

Fluency

- Ask "How many circus words can you think of in two minutes?"

- Find out how many students in the class have been to the circus.

- Ask them to list the types of acts they saw.

- Have students list all the people associated with the circus. Remind them that there are many behind-the-scenes people, such as those who look after the animals, those who make the costumes, and those who sell food and tickets.

- Ask students to list five books about the circus.

Flexibility

- Ask students to separate the list of circus people into different categories such as funny acts, dangerous acts, and so on.

- Have students describe what a juggler does.

- Ask "What sort of things would an acrobat need to know?"

- Have students write a story from the point of view of a clown who is performing for the first time in a circus act.

Originality

- Have students describe the act that a flame-eating trapeze artist would perform. Ask them for other funny combinations.

- Ask them to list all the ways to make a clown laugh and a crowd cheer.

- Have students use an umbrella, a shopping cart, and a banana to create a brand new circus act.

- Have students describe what a circus will look like 100 years from now.

- Have students design a flag for a circus.

- Ask students to invent a story which tells about a heroic act by a tightrope-walker.

Elaboration

- Have students list ten different uses for a circus tent.

- Have students apply for a job as a clown.

- Ask "If you could join a circus, what is the one thing you would most like to do? Why is this your favorite?"

- Have students work in pairs to create a way to make the game of *Chutes and Ladders* into an exciting circus act.

- Have students start a story with this beginning: "It was my first visit to the circus. I was very excited. Suddenly the crowd became quiet. I looked up and could not believe my eyes…"

Creative Thinking in English

The Circus

It is good to have animal acts in a circus.
What do you think?
List five good things and
five bad things about
having animals in a circus.

Clowns

How could a clown
use these to be funny?
An old shoe
A box
A loaf of bread

Elephants

Make up five questions
for this answer:
An elephant,

What do you think?

What do a *juggler*
and a *computer*
have in common?

Creative Thinking in English

Magic Trick

Invent a magic trick to perform for your friends.

A New Machine

Design a machine which could put up and take down the circus tent all by itself.

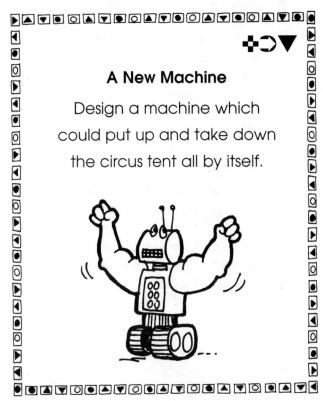

An Unusual Circus Act

Make up a circus act that could be performed by Jack, the beanstalk, and the giant.

A Balancing Act

Use these materials to construct something that a tightrope walker could use in a circus act:

A newspaper

A wheelbarrow

2 balloons

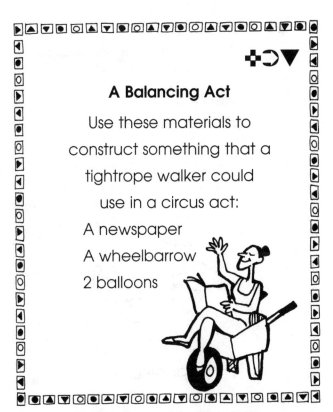

Creative Thinking in Math

Encourage students' creative thinking in math by beginning each lesson with a quick challenge related to the unit of work they are about to study. This will focus students' thinking and encourage active participation in the lesson right from the start. It will also help to create a more positive attitude towards the learning process.

Fluency

Encourage students to think about the thinking skills and inquiry processes required for solving problems. Encourage them to brainstorm ideas and come up with a lot of solutions and possibilities. Stimulate discussion with problems like these:

- List as many round things as you can in two minutes.

- List all the possible uses for a ruler.

- Can you name all the objects with angles in the classroom?

- List all the objects in the classroom that are different solid shapes. For example, a pencil is a cylinder shape.

Flexibility

Expand brainstorming activities by adapting and extending them. Suggestions follow:

- Group the words brainstormed about shapes into as many different categories as you can, for example, big and little, smooth and rough, solid and hollow.

- Have students think of some new uses for a fifty-cent piece.

- Compare a cube to a sphere. How are they the same? How are they different?

- Ask students to think of reasons why coins are round. Ask them to suggest other shapes they could be. Discuss the problems and benefits.

Originality

Encourage originality by asking open-ended questions, providing students with more opportunities to think in the abstract and rewarding creative and innovative solutions. Suggest the following to the students:

- Pair up and then design a math puzzle for your partner to solve.

- Invent new names for the days of the week.

- Imagine you are only 30 centimeters tall. How would the world be different?

- Design a new shape for a milk carton.

- What would our houses look like if they had no corners?

Elaboration

Have students work in groups or individually to reflect upon the previous three processes. Ask them to look at alternatives, expand on ideas, and add more details with activities such as those suggested below:

- Draw a triangle shape. Add details to make it into a soft toy.

- Add to the number 5 to make it into an interesting pattern.

- You have won $50. You have to spend it all on your dog. Describe how you would spend your money.

- Imagine what would happen if the bat in baseball was changed to a box shape and the ball to a pyramid shape. Describe how the game would change.

Creative Thinking in Math

Space

Make a train like the one shown,
using cylinders of different sizes.

How many cylinders make your train?

Measurement

Name something that takes longer than:

Eating an ice cream cone _____

Making your bed _____

Brushing your teeth _____

Time

Name the three months of summer.

_____

_____

_____

Draw a summer picture on a separate
piece of paper.

Name:

Management
Strategies:

Shapes

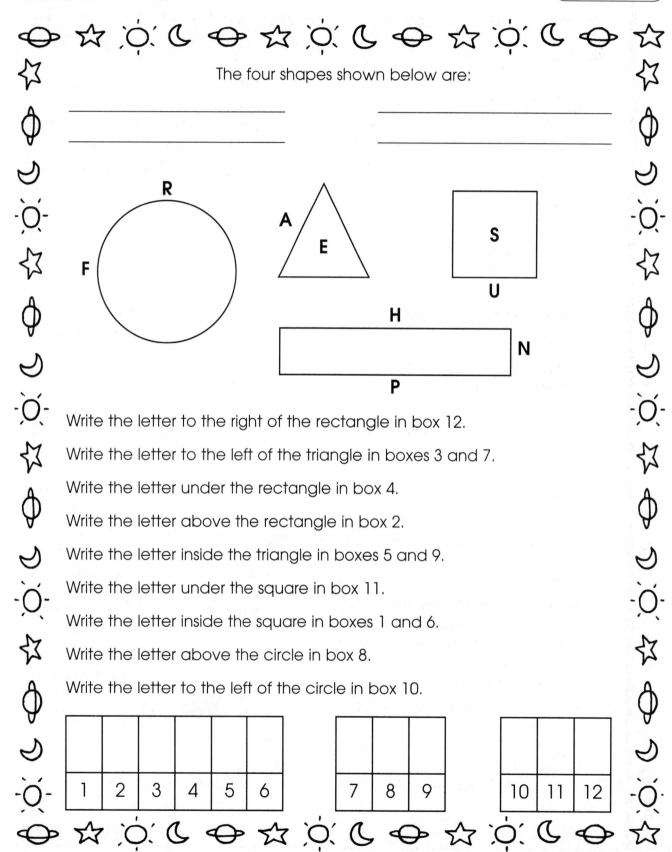

The four shapes shown below are:

_____   _____

_____   _____

R

A

E

S

U

F

H

N

P

Write the letter to the right of the rectangle in box 12.

Write the letter to the left of the triangle in boxes 3 and 7.

Write the letter under the rectangle in box 4.

Write the letter above the rectangle in box 2.

Write the letter inside the triangle in boxes 5 and 9.

Write the letter under the square in box 11.

Write the letter inside the square in boxes 1 and 6.

Write the letter above the circle in box 8.

Write the letter to the left of the circle in box 10.

1	2	3	4	5	6

7	8	9

10	11	12

Creative Thinking in Science

Theme: Pets

Fluency

- Have students list all the animals they have as pets.

- Ask students to name five animals that are extinct. What are five questions you would have liked to ask one of the extinct animals?

- Ask students which animals make the best pets? Why?

- Have students list the types of foods their pets eat.

- Ask students to list animals which would not make good pets. Why?

Flexibility

- Have students work out three different ways to clean a dirty dog without using water.

- Find common points between a mouse and a cup of coffee.

- Say "Convince your parents that a hippopotamus would make a great pet."

- Classify the list of pets into big and little. Ask students to group them in other ways.

- Ask "Do you think animals can talk to each other? Observe a group of animals. What sounds do they make? What do you think the sounds mean? How could you talk to animals?"

- Ask students the pros and cons of being a dog.

- Have students compare a polar bear to an opossum. How are they alike? How are they different?

Originality

- Ask students how and where they could hide an elephant.

- Say "You have lots of pet mice to give away. Think of ways to convince people a mouse would make the best pet in the world."

- Have students pretend that they are a goldfish. Ask them to describe what life is like inside a goldfish bowl.

- Say "If all the animals decided to rule the world, which animal would be the leader? Why?"

- Plan a *Pet Day* for the class. Have students work in groups allocated to planning different sections of the day, for example, the timetable, the list of pets, invitations.

Elaboration

- Have students decide which would be the best animal to have as a class pet. Ask them to justify their choices"

- Ask "What if you had a broken leg and couldn't take your dog for a walk? How many other ways could you exercise it?"

- Ask students to choose whether they would rather be a giraffe or a green tree frog and give reasons for their answers.

- Say "If you could be any animal in the world, which animal would you choose? Give at least five reasons for your choice."

Creative Thinking in Science

A Different Dog Kennel

Draw a dog house.
Can you make it different by
making one part bigger,
adding something extra,
or replacing one part with
something else?

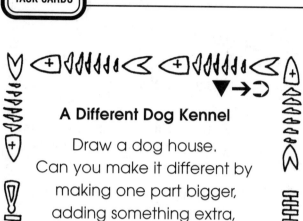

Pet Goldfish

Can you design a collar
for a goldfish?

My Pet Shark

Sharks would make
excellent pets.
List three good points
and three bad points
for this idea.

An Ideal Pet

Create an animal that can
fly, swim, walk, climb,
carry you for long distances
and would make
an ideal pet.

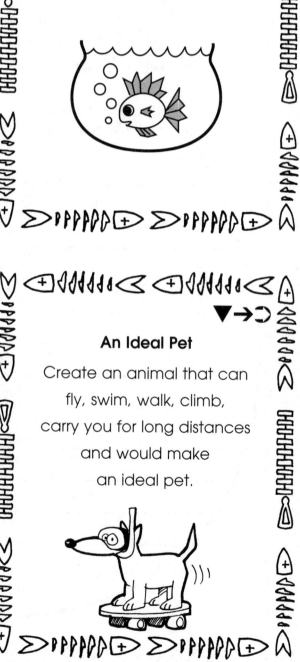

Name: _____

CREATIVE THINKING

Science

BLM 15

Life in a Goldfish Bowl

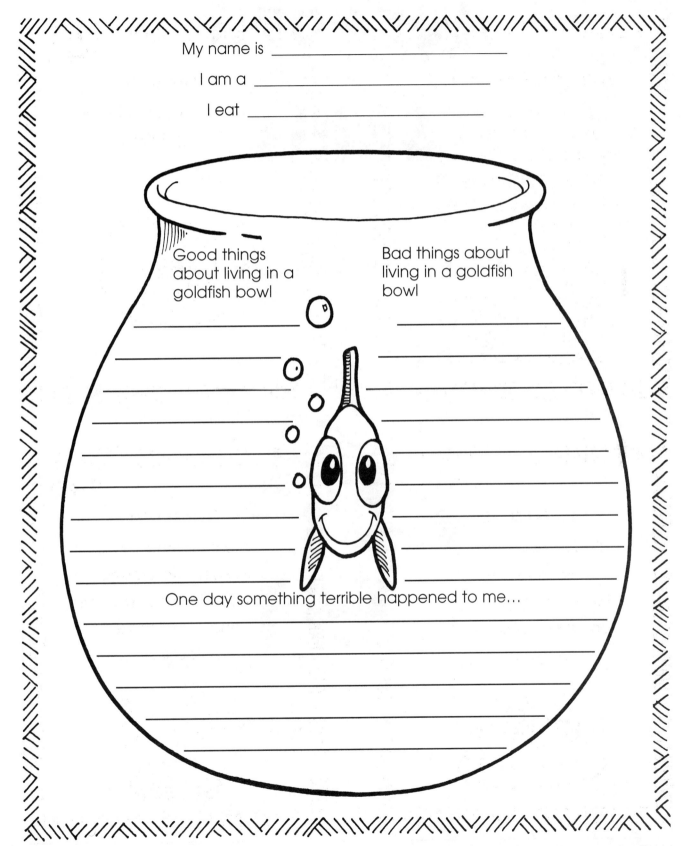

My name is _____

I am a _____

I eat _____

Good things about living in a goldfish bowl

Bad things about living in a goldfish bowl

One day something terrible happened to me...

Research Skills

Notes and Activities

by Rosalind Curtis

Overview for the Classroom Teacher

Research Skills

Research skills are needed by all students so that they can analyze and interpret information that is presented to them. Information can be presented to students by means of written text, visual input (pictures, videos, computer terminal), aural input (listening to speakers, radio, sounds within the environment), and kinesthetic input (through senses of touch, taste, and smell).

Research skills that need to be taught to students are the following:

Questioning techniques help students clarify issues, problems, and decisions when looking at a topic.

Developing planning frameworks that will assist students to access prior knowledge and identify sources of information which will help build further knowledge and understanding.

Gathering strategies help students collect and store information for later consideration, for example note-taking, identifying main ideas, and text clarification.

Sorting strategies help students to prioritize and organize information by using retrieval charts and sequencing information, for example.

Synthesizing skills help students take the original information and reorganize it in order to develop decisions and solutions.

Evaluation helps the students to determine if the information found is sufficient to support a solution or conclusion.

Reporting skills allow the students to translate findings into persuasive, instructive, and effective products, including the presentation of a project.

These research skills are best taught within the classroom by means of a **research cycle**. This cycle provides students with the steps to plan and conduct meaningful research to complete projects, solve problems, and make informed decisions.

① Students **explore** a variety of sources to gather information.

⑦ After completion of analysis, students will **combine** their findings to create their final projects.

② Students **identify** information sources that will contain data to help with their decision.

⑥ Students **ask** themselves why this information is important and how it will affect their decisions.

③ Once information is found **decisions** must be made about which data to keep.

⑤ Students begin to **analyze** their data by establishing criteria that will help them reach a decision.

④ Students **sort** information to enable them to categorize and organize their findings so that analysis can begin.

Overview for the Classroom Teacher

The Research Cycle

There are seven steps in the research cycle.

1 Questioning

- This step identifies the problem that needs solving.

- Students need to be taught questioning skills which will enable them to identify what data is needed to solve the main problem. It is critical that students are encouraged to think laterally and from as many perspectives as possible.

- From the questioning process, students should be able to identify information they already know and formulate questions to locate information they need to find out.

2 Planning

- This step begins to develop information-seeking strategies to help locate answers to all the questions asked.

- Students need to be introduced to the range of resources which are available, such as books, videos, people, pictures and the Internet.

- Students need to plan how to organize the information that will be gathered.

3 Gathering

- This step enables students to clarify the information that has been located.

- Students need to develop effective note-taking strategies so that the main idea is identified from the information.

- Students also need to recognize the value of a bibliography so that they may return to an information source, if required.

4 Sorting

- This step requires students to systematically scan the data for relevant information that will contribute to understanding.

- Students need to classify the gathered information under headings and sub-headings and make generalizations about it.

- The data gathered can then be placed into a sequence of events.

5 Synthesizing

- This process is like doing a jigsaw puzzle.

- Students need to arrange and rearrange fragments of information until patterns begin to emerge.

- Students develop their skills so that they are able to answer questions with understanding, accuracy and detail.

6 Evaluation

- When this stage is first reached, early attempts to synthesize information may result in the need for more information to clarify or enhance understanding. If the students find that pieces are missing, they will need to begin the cycle again or ask what more is needed to complete their picture.

- As the cycle begins again, questioning will become more specific and will lead to more planning and more gathering of information.

- When the picture seems to be complete, the students can decide that the cycle should finish.

- It may be necessary to repeat the cycle and gather more information until the students decide that an investigation is complete.

7 Reporting

- After the cycle has been completed, it is time to report and share findings. This may take the form of an oral, written, or graphic presentation, a debate, or any other presentation that students may decide upon.

Classroom Design

- Have students work independently or in mixed-ability or homogeneous groups, as appropriate to the activity.

- Provide a variety of resources around the room, including hands-on, extension, and learning center activities aimed at different levels.

- Always give a criteria for marking and a timeline for work to be completed.

Research Skills in English

Theme: Health and Sport

Questioning

- Have students look at a picture of an athlete. Have them ask questions like:

  What is this person doing? (factual)

  What did this person do to win the event? (inferential)

  If this person is a member of a team, what things did they have to do to win? (creative)

  Do you think this person could have performed better on the day? Why? (critical)

- Have students devise questions to find out the class's favorite food.

Planning

- Ask students to write down different sources of information about food, for example, cookbooks, magazines, recipe cards.

- Identify words that could be used to search on the Internet for a sport (tennis, Wimbledon, Pete Sampras) or food (health, recipes, diet).

- Model a mind map on the board and then have students draw their own mind maps for a sport.

Gathering

- Ask students to bring in newspapers, magazines, or catalogs that have pictures of sports equipment, athletes, and different types of food.

- Have students watch a video about famous athletes and then draw or write down important facts about one of them.

- Have students list a variety of different manufactured health foods such as muesli bars and cereals.

- Have students visit Websites such as **www.ausport.govt.au** to locate sporting information.

Sorting

- Model how to sort foods according to different attributes like snack foods and wholesome foods. Ask students to regroup the information in many different ways, for example, milk, fruit, nuts.

- Have students organize information under headings in their sports mind maps so that they can identify data which is important to them.

Synthesizing

- Have students use the information they have gathered to help them identify the important habits of a good athlete, for example, a healthy diet.

- Have students draw a cartoon strip about how a particular athlete became famous.

- Ask students to role-play this person performing a winning moment in the sport.

Evaluating

- Have students give reasons why a particular food is good for them.

- Ask students to choose their favorite athlete. Ask them to explain why they think their particular person is better than any other famous athlete.

- Ask students to write a recipe using their favorite food. Is this food healthy?

Reporting

- Have students present a one-minute oral report to convince the class that their favorite athlete is the greatest ever.

- Ask students to write a story or use pictures to tell about meeting their famous athlete.

- Have students write a jingle about their favorite healthy food.

Name:

Management
Strategies:

Food

Sorting, Analyzing

TASK 1: Draw a picture of each food.

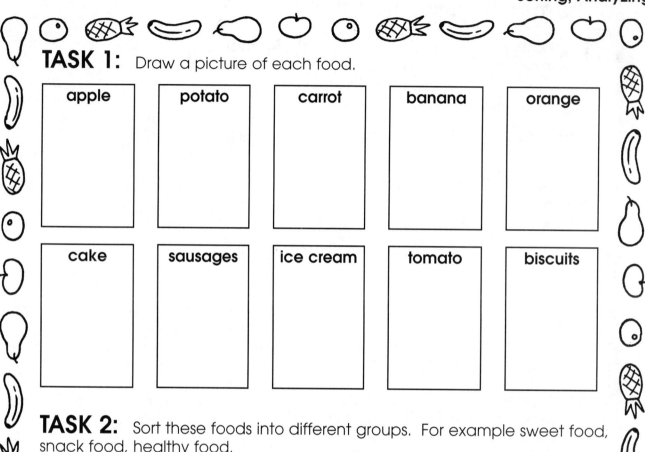

apple	potato	carrot	banana	orange
cake	sausages	ice cream	tomato	biscuits

TASK 2: Sort these foods into different groups. For example sweet food, snack food, healthy food.

Sweet Food	Snack Food	Healthy Food

Name: _____

Management
Strategies:

RESEARCH
SKILLS

English

BLM 17

Famous Sports People

Synthesizing, Evaluating

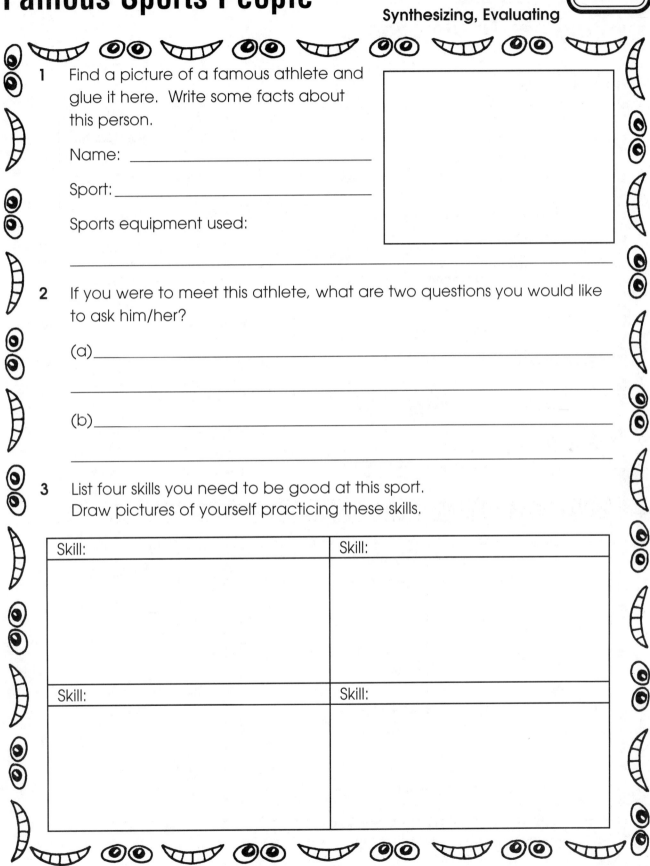

1 Find a picture of a famous athlete and glue it here. Write some facts about this person.

Name: _____

Sport: _____

Sports equipment used:

_____

2 If you were to meet this athlete, what are two questions you would like to ask him/her?

(a) _____

_____

(b) _____

_____

3 List four skills you need to be good at this sport.
   Draw pictures of yourself practicing these skills.

Skill:	Skill:
Skill:	Skill:

Research Skills for Math

Theme: Numeration

Questioning

- Ask students questions such as these about how numbers are written:
- What do we call the symbols that we use to count with?
- How is the position of each number important?
- What does 437 mean? Can I write it in a different way?
- Have students identify different words related to numeration, such as place value, ones, tens, hundreds. Ask them to explain how these relate to the way numbers are represented.

Planning

- Have students verbalize the steps they will take in deciding how to represent a group of counters or a bundle of sticks.
- Ask students how place value could be represented in a number like 437.
- Have students write down or verbalize any information or processes they already know that could help them solve a problem. For example, "I know that 16 can be written as 1 ten and 6 ones."

Gathering

- Ask students to try all the different ways that they can think of to represent 999.
- Have students compare different answers to the same problem. For example,
  $3 + 3 = 4 + 2 = 5 + 1 = 7 - 1$.
- Ask students to find pictures to represent the same numbers (a picture with 5 dogs, a sentence with 5 words, 5 tally marks).

Sorting

- Have students organize numbers in ascending and descending order.
- Have students organize a group of numbers such as 48, 4, 473, and 41 from lowest to highest.

Synthesizing

- Have students represent numbers in many different ways, for example pictures, symbols, or different number sentences.
- Have students develop patterns using place value and repetition of number patterns.
- Have students use numeration to devise problems for the class to solve, for example, "Is 51 higher than 510?"

Evaluating

- Ask students to check whether given answers to an algorithm have correct place value and have them explain why.
- Give students some information and have them explain whether it is correct or incorrect. Have them provide reasons for their decisions. For example, "Is 327 made up of 3 tens, 2 hundreds and 7 ones?"

Reporting

- Ask students to present an oral report on how they went about solving a math problem. Make sure that they verbalize all the steps taken and give reasons for why they solved the problem in that particular way.
- Have students present a dramatization of a number sentence such as, "Three birds were sitting on a tree, two more joined them, and that made five."

Name:

Representing Numbers

We can represent the number 12 using pictures and number sentences:

12 ⊛⊛⊛⊛⊛⊛⊛⊛⊛⊛ ⊛⊛	12 ☆☆☆☆ ❀❀❀❀ ❄❄❄❄
10 + 2	4 + 4 + 4

Think of two more ways to represent the number 12.

12	12

TASK: Use pictures and number sentences to represent the numbers 11, 15, and 18 in as many different ways as you can.

11	15	18

Research Skills in Math

RESEARCH SKILLS
Math
TASK CARDS

Graphs

Make a graph of class members for two attributes such as eye color and hair color. Present your findings in a variety of ways. For example, pie graphs, bar graphs or picture graphs.

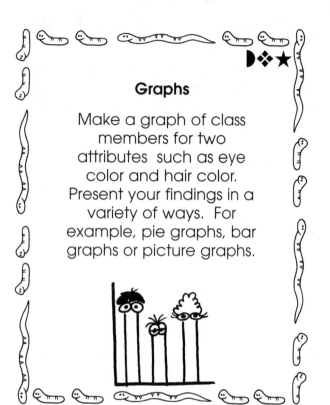

Estimation

Estimate how many of these will fit along the board:
- books
- pieces of chalk
- pencils

How can you check your answer without putting the things onto the board?

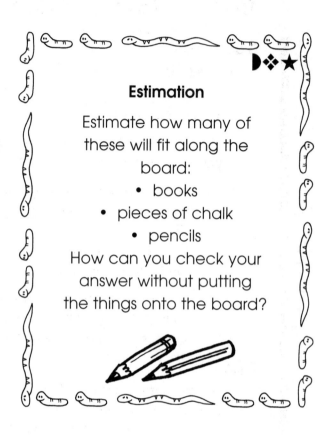

Constructing a Bridge

Show how ten different sized boxes could be used to construct a bridge.

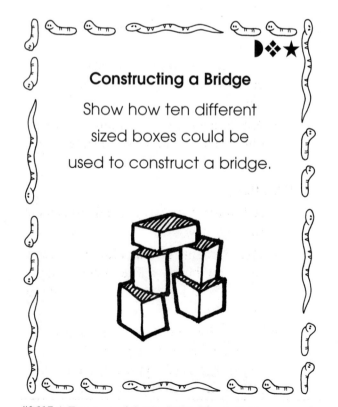

Triangles

Use a triangle and one other shape to completely fill a space of 20 cm by 10 cm.

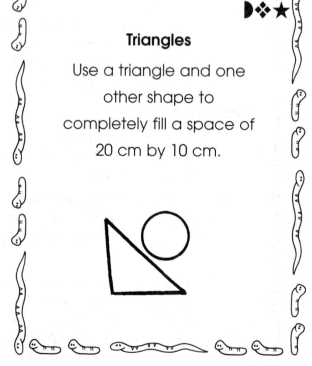

Research Skills in Social Studies

Theme: Toys and Games

Questioning

- Have students question given statements such as these:

  We need toys to help us learn.

  Toys are better today than when our parents were children.

- Ask students to devise the questions that go with given answers, for example,

  "If the answer is Snakes and Ladders, what could the question be?"

- Have students make up questions for surveys to gauge opinions on using electronic games versus board games.

Planning

- Ask students to identify those resources which might have information for further research into toys and games (books, toy stores, grandparents, Internet).

- Ask students to write down what information they know and what they wish to find out about toys and games such as indoor games, outdoor games, materials used to make toys.

Gathering

- Have students select a game or toy and write down what they think are its good and bad points.

- Ask students to bring in books, magazines, and pictures of a variety of toys so that they can examine many different types.

- Have students visit Websites such as *www.historychannel.com* to find out about the history of toys and games.

Sorting

- Have students find all different types of wheels, feet, wings, and springs that can be found on toys and sort them according to various attributes such as size, shape, and usefulness.

- Give students a list of games and ask them to prioritize them from most to least enjoyable.

- Ask students to match games and rules, for example, baseball with home run.

Synthesizing

- Ask students to describe a new toy in a letter to a friend.

- Have students make suggestions about how to improve a game.

- Ask students to devise a new toy.

Evaluating

- Have students explain why they think their new toy will be better than any other toy.

- Ask students to give reasons for their choices and to explain why they will work.

- Ask students to give comments about other students' toys and to state whether they would buy them.

Reporting

- Ask students to write an advertisement for their new toy.

- Have students give an oral or written report on their toy. The intent of the report should be to persuade people to buy the toy.

- As a major activity, have students design their ideal new school. Encourage them to present their schools as a variety of models.

Name:

A New toy

Sorting, Evaluating

Develop a new toy that has wheels, wings, feet, and springs.

In the spaces below write how many of each item your toy will have and draw what each part will look like.

Wheels	Wings	Feet	Springs

My toy will be called: _____

This is what my toy can do: _____

_____

_____

Draw how you and your friends could use this toy.

The best thing about this toy is: _____

_____

Name:

A Different School

Gathering, Synthesizing, Evaluating

Design a new school. You can decide what the school will be called and what subjects are to be taught.

My new school will be called _____

This is what my new school will look like.

These subjects will be taught. | Schedule

I would like these subjects because _____

_____

_____

_____

Important school rules:

1 _____

2 _____

3 _____

4 _____

Questioning Skills and Brainstorming

Notes and Activities

by Fay Holbert

Overview for the Classroom Teacher

Questioning Skills

Generally speaking, 30% of class time is taken up in questioning (that is about 100 questions per hour). In most classrooms 85% of questions are asked by the teacher, and 90% of those do no more than demand memory or recall by the students. Therefore, teachers should aim to use more open-ended and divergent questions to improve the students' creative thinking and problem-solving abilities.

Questioning Guidelines for the Teacher:

1. Maintain a high level of enthusiasm.

2. Accept that individual differences in students will determine how, what, how much, and how fast learning occurs.

3. Encourage divergent thinking.

4. Avoid all forms of "put-downs". Be positive! Say "Great!" "Good try!" "Tell me more!" "I've never thought of it like that!"

5. Try to minimize "Who?" "What?" "Where?" and maximize "Why?" and "How?"

Bloom's Taxonomy emphasizes the idea that with brighter students, more time should be devoted to the higher level activities and objectives. Knowledge and comprehension deal with facts, figures, definitions, and rules, which all students need to know. However, teachers should encourage the brighter students (who will generally grasp new information quickly and comprehend more rapidly) to do the following:

- *Apply* this knowledge.

- *Analyze* components, relationships, and hypotheses.

- *Synthesize* these components into creative solutions, plans, and theories.

- *Evaluate* the accuracy, value, and efficiency of alternative ideas or actions.

Examples of questions which help to apply knowledge:

When did . . . ?

Can you list . . . ?

Which action/event was the cause of . . . ?

Can you give an example of . . . ?

How would you have . . . ?

Why was . . . ?

Examples of questions which help to analyze knowledge:

Why did . . . do this?

Can you sequence . . . ?

Examples of questions which help to synthesize knowledge:

How would this situation have changed if . . . ?

What if the "bears" had been "monkeys?"

Examples of questions which help to evaluate knowledge:

How could . . . have been improved?

Who do you think has the strongest character? Why?

Overview for the Classroom Teacher

Brainstorming

Another technique which encourages creative thinking is **brainstorming**.

The aim of brainstorming is to develop a safe, non-judgmental setting where all students feel confident and eager to participate in the lesson.

It was Alex Osborn who identified some valuable conditions and rules for brainstorming. The main principle is deferred judgment. This means that idea evaluation is postponed until later. Osborn stressed that any kind of criticism or evaluation interferes with the generation of imaginative ideas simply because it is very difficult to do both at the same time.

It is important for the teacher to remind the students of the basic rules of brainstorming:

1. No criticism is allowed no matter how irrelevant or preposterous the responses may appear to be.

2. A substantial quantity of ideas is required. The more ideas you have, the more likely it is that you will have motivated all students to contribute, and thus it is more likely that you will find good solutions.

3. Accept and record all answers. To begin with, it is perhaps easier for the teacher to be the scribe, but when brainstorming is a regular feature of the class's activities, students can record responses.

4. Eliminate any stiffness or inflexibility. Be open to alternatives.

5. If responses slack off, add your own. The teacher's role is to keep urging: "What else could we do?" "Who else has an idea?" The teacher may even specifically direct questions to a group of quieter students.

6. Link ideas wherever possible. Ask questions such as "How can we express this more clearly?" "Could we improve this one?" "What if we put these three ideas together?"

7. Encourage fantasy, imagination, and lateral thinking.

8. Encourage cooperative work among students.

9. If there were a school problem (for example, the sudden appearance of graffiti on the school playground), the students could be given 24-hours' notice so that all have an opportunity to discuss this at home and be prepared to brainstorm a solution for the next day. Brighter students soon learn to organize and lead group brainstorming sessions.

Some variations of brainstorming are:

Reverse brainstorming: This technique quickly points out what is currently being done incorrectly and implicitly suggests specific solutions. For example, "How can we increase vandalism?"

Stop-and-Go Brainstorming: Short periods of approximately 6 – 8 minutes of brainstorming are interspersed with evaluation. The evaluation sheets help keep the group on target by selecting the most profitable directions to pursue.

Phillips 66: This is a technique using small groups of 6. Students brainstorm for 6 minutes and then a member of each group reports the best, or all ideas to the larger group.

Questioning Skills and Brainstorming for English

Theme: People Who Help in the Community

Knowledge

- Teacher-led discussion can ascertain that all students understand the concept of a community.
- Brainstorm:
  What is a community? What makes up a community? Who are some important people who help make my community a better and safer place to live?
- Find out how many students know the emergency telephone number (911). Write this number in the classroom in an obvious location for all to see and memorize.

Comprehension

- Ask students what they understand by the term "call out," as associated with emergency situations.
- Ask: "How can you tell when someone is responding to a call out?"
- From the brainstorming list of "Important People in Our Community," have students identify the ones who help us to save lives.
- Ask "Why do these people need fast vehicles?"
- Brainstorm: "How do police officers help us? How do paramedics help us? How do fire fighters help us?"

Application

- Give students several emergency scenarios, such as their house being on fire. Ask them how they would react in each circumstance.
- Have students work in groups of 4 to 5 to role-play the rescuers and rescued in some of these emergency scenarios.
- Pose the question: "Are there differences among the sirens that the police, ambulance, and fire vehicles use? Why?"

Analysis

- Ask "Can you list the skills that a police officer, a paramedic, and a fire fighter would need to be able to perform their duties well?"
- Brainstorm: "How can you avoid accidents that need the attention of these people?"
- Ask "Why do you think uniforms are worn by these people while they are on duty?"
- Have the students categorize the many different types of duties that the above three community helpers are called upon to perform. For example, police may catch criminals, look for missing persons, or present talks at schools.

Synthesis

Pose such questions as:

- What would you do if the paramedics were already busy at a major emergency when you called for them to come? Who else could you call for help?
- What happens to people who live in small, remote communities when they are in need of urgent medical help? Have students choose some of these scenarios to role-play.
- How could you help police officers, paramedics and fire fighters to do their jobs? How can we get to know more about the work that these people do?
- Plan a display of People Who Help in Our Community for the classroom or school library. Students can design posters and collect pictures, brochures, and newspaper articles which show how each of these organizations are structured.

Evaluation

- Ask "What would it be like to have none of these men and women available to us for a whole day?"
- List ways that people in our community show their appreciation for the work that these people do. For example, they can write to thank them for their hard work in the community.

Name:

People Who Help in the Community

Application, Synthesis

TASK 1: Draw some of the equipment these community helpers use.

Fire Fighters	Police Officers	Paramedics

TASK 2: Draw an emergency where all three of the above community helpers have been called upon to work together.

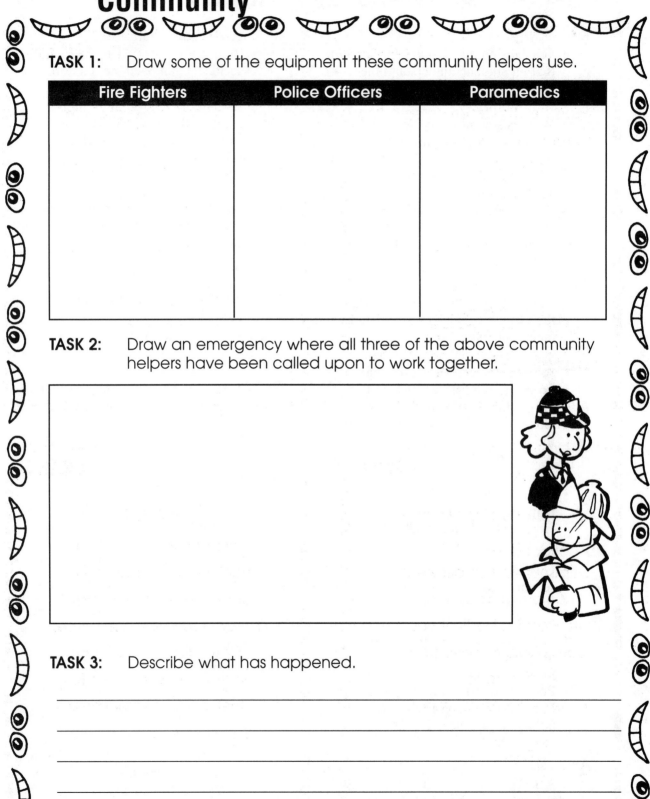

TASK 3: Describe what has happened.

_____

_____

_____

_____

Questioning Skills and Brainstorming for English

Application, Analysis, Evaluation

Asking Questions

Prepare three interesting questions you would like to ask the officers at your local:

- police station
- fire station
- paramedic station

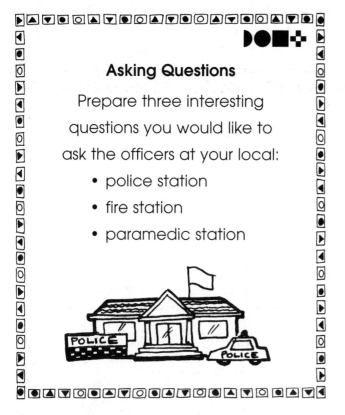

Road Rules

Work in a small group to set up a "busy intersection" in your school playground. Take turns to act as pedestrians, cyclists, car drivers, and traffic officers to make sure that everyone knows road and safety rules.

Shortest Route

On a map of your community, use different colors to trace the shortest routes that you could take to drive from home to:

- the paramedic station
- the police station
- the fire station.

The Future

Design new tools and vehicles that each of our community helpers might be able to use in the future. Draw diagrams of your inventions with labels for their parts. Explain how your inventions would work.

© Teacher Created Materials, Inc. 61 #3617 A Treasury of Critical Thinking Activities

Questioning Skills and Brainstorming for Math

Theme: Shapes

Introduction

- Display diagrams of shapes: squares, triangles (equilateral, isosceles, scalene), oblong, rectangle, hexagon.
- Write the above words on the board. Also add diamond, straight, curved, parallel, round, oval, angle, right angle, quadrilateral. Point to the shapes to help explain each of these features.

Knowledge

- Ask students to name the displayed shapes as they are indicated by the teacher.
- Have students explain the properties of each shape.
- Have students write the words on the board to illustrate the new vocabulary they have learned.

Comprehension

- Brainstorm: How many square, triangular, rectangular, circular, and hexagonal shapes can you find

  in the classroom?

  at home?

  outdoors?

- Give students cardboard cutouts of the above shapes in many different sizes and colors. Have students place them in their appropriate groups.

Application

- Ask "What could you use to draw a circle?" Have students demonstrate their ideas.
- Have students print the alphabet in 3 groups of shapes:
- those letters with all straight lines
- those letters with all curved lines
- those letters with both straight and curved lines.
- Pose the question: "How could you form an exact right angle by folding a piece of paper?" Allow students to experiment.

Analysis

- Ask "What is common in all the above shapes except the circle?" Have students work in groups to list suggestions and report back to the class.
- Have the students investigate what makes a square different from

  an oblong.

  any other quadrilateral.

- Ask "Why is the circle different from all the other shapes?"

Synthesis

To stimulate synthesizing activities, pose open-ended questions such as those listed below, and encourage students to experiment:

- What shapes could you draw if you only had a piece of string and a pencil?
- Why is it easier to use a tool which has a round handle rather than a square one?
- What difficulties would we face if we had triangular television screens?
- Why do you think steps are usually rectangular?

Evaluation

- Organize an excursion to the local supermarket. Have the students note the most common shapes of goods on the shelves and report their findings back to the class. (Students can also use the school cafeteria as an alternative source.)
- Ask students to find out the most common type of line (straight, curved, zigzag) used in constructing a building.
- Pose this question: "What are the most common shapes seen in the structure of a house?" Have students present an oral or written report to the class on their findings.

Questioning Skills and Brainstorming for Math

Application

Money

Draw in detail a coin which is not circular in shape.   How many sides does it have?   Why isn't this coin minted as a circular shape like the others?

Square Wheels

Draw your bicycle with square wheels. Explain how this would affect the way the bicycle travels.

Paper Squares

Collect two paper squares.

Fold the first square once. You now have a _____ shape.

Fold it again. You now have a _____ shape.

How many different shapes can you get if you fold the paper in a different way?

Questioning Skills and Brainstorming for Math

Analysis, Synthesis, Evaluation

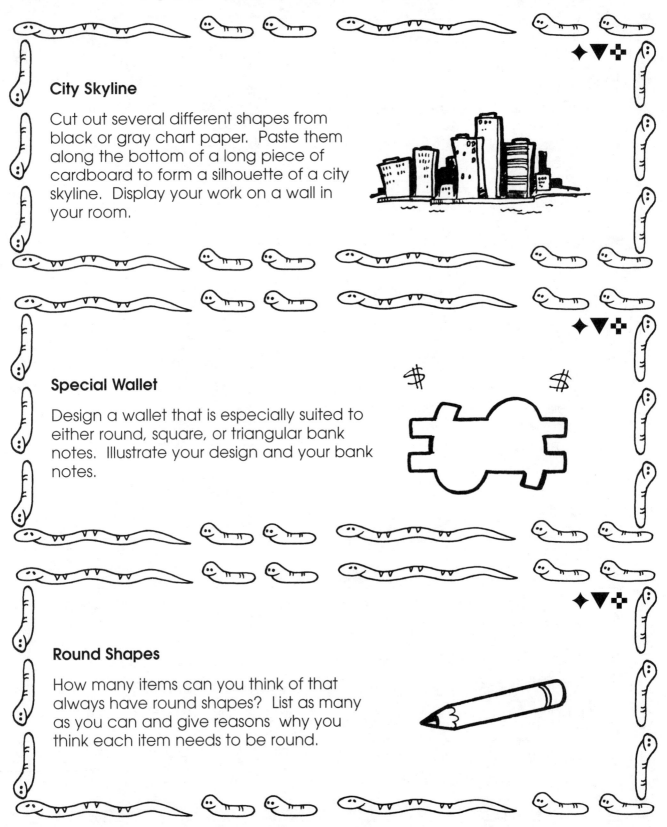

City Skyline

Cut out several different shapes from black or gray chart paper. Paste them along the bottom of a long piece of cardboard to form a silhouette of a city skyline. Display your work on a wall in your room.

Special Wallet

Design a wallet that is especially suited to either round, square, or triangular bank notes. Illustrate your design and your bank notes.

Round Shapes

How many items can you think of that always have round shapes? List as many as you can and give reasons why you think each item needs to be round.

Questioning Skills and Brainstorming for Science

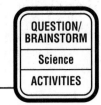

Theme: The Skeleton

Introduction
- Display a picture of a human skeleton for students to identify to ensure that all are comfortable with the term.

Knowledge
- Say "Name any bones of the skeleton and point to each bone you name on the diagram of the skeleton." (For this age group "shin," "upper arm," "ribs" are acceptable.)
- Reverse brainstorm with students: "What would happen if we didn't have a skeleton?" Its importance should quickly become clear.
- Ask "Which bones are often broken by children? Why is this so?"
- Ask "What are joints? What do our joints do?" Encourage students to name all their joints and investigate their flexibility of movement.

Comprehension
- Brainstorm "What special work do the skull and the ribs do for us?"
- Have students look at their hands. Ask "How many bones do you think there are in your hand? (27) How many in each finger (4) and thumb (3)?"
- Pose this question "Which other joints in your body operate like your fingers?" Compare this with the action of a hinge on a door. Encourage students to name other similar objects.
- Ask "Which joints can you name that do not work like hinges? Why is this difference necessary?"

Application
- Prepare thick cardboard cutout shapes of the main sections of the skeleton, such as the skull, rib cage, arms, legs, pelvis, and spine. Have students reassemble the skeleton using blu-tack, fine wire, and split pins.
- Pose these questions: "Why do we need so many bones?

What can we do to help strengthen our bones? How are you able to move your arms, legs, and head? Why do we have skin to cover our skeletons?"

Analysis
Encourage students to analyze with questions such as these:
- What would happen if we had just one long bone in our leg or arm or back?
- Why do we need so many bones in our wrists and hands, ankles and feet?
- What happens when a person breaks a bone? How is it treated? How long does it take to mend? Encourage students to recount any personal experiences with broken bones.

Synthesis
- Encourage students to find out what equipment is available to help protect their bones while they play sports. Have them name sports they play where it is advisable to wear this protective equipment.
- Ask "In what ways are skeletons of other creatures similar to or different from the human skeleton?" Have them compare and contrast the skeletons of a variety of land and sea creatures, for example, a snake that has only a vertebrae, or a worm which has no bones, or a crab which has its "skeleton" on the outside.

Evaluation
- Have students make a list of all sports where protective equipment should be compulsory for all players to wear. Ask them to provide reasons for their choices.
- Ask "How could we make games safer for young people to play?"
- Invite a nurse, doctor or paramedic to speak to your class about the human skeleton. Encourage students to prepare a list of questions to ask.

Name:

The Human Skeleton

In the boxes below draw the bones of

a) the arm and hand

b) the leg and foot.

Choose the correct words from those below to label each bone and joint:

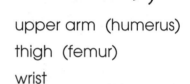

forearm (radius and ulna)	upper arm (humerus)
lower leg (tibia and fibula)	thigh (femur)
kneecap (patella)	wrist
ankle	knee
elbow	knuckles

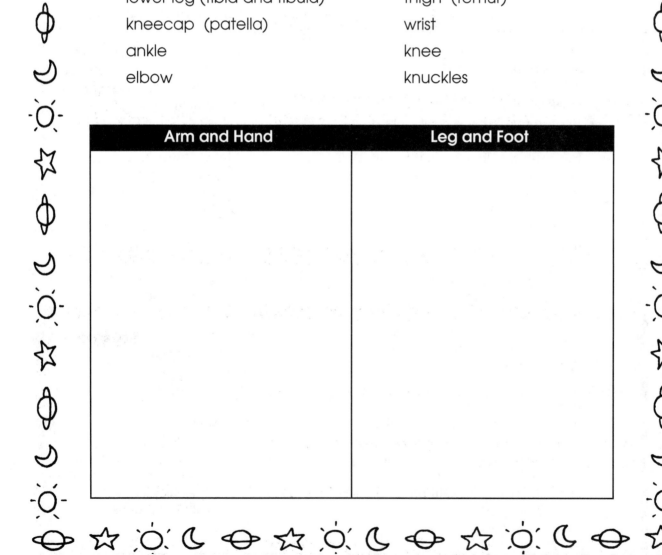

Arm and Hand	Leg and Foot

Questioning Skills and Brainstorming for Science

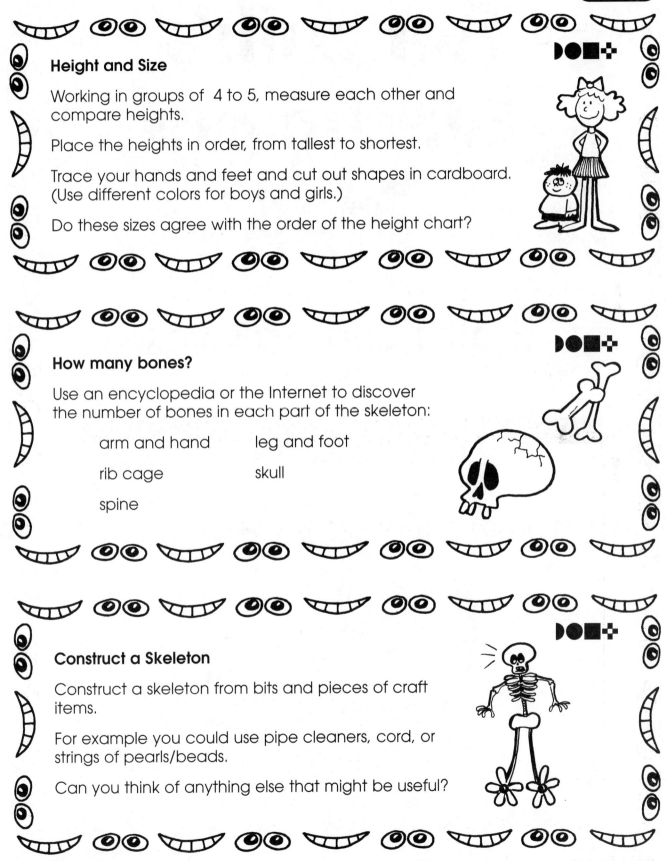

Height and Size

Working in groups of 4 to 5, measure each other and compare heights.

Place the heights in order, from tallest to shortest.

Trace your hands and feet and cut out shapes in cardboard. (Use different colors for boys and girls.)

Do these sizes agree with the order of the height chart?

How many bones?

Use an encyclopedia or the Internet to discover the number of bones in each part of the skeleton:

arm and hand   leg and foot

rib cage   skull

spine

Construct a Skeleton

Construct a skeleton from bits and pieces of craft items.

For example you could use pipe cleaners, cord, or strings of pearls/beads.

Can you think of anything else that might be useful?

Renzulli's Enrichment Triad

Notes and Activities

by Rosalind Curtis

Overview for the Classroom Teacher

RENZULLI'S TRIAD

NOTES

Introduction to Renzulli's Enrichment Triad Model

The Enrichment Triad Model was devised by Joseph Renzulli in 1983 as a framework to provide students with the skills to carry out their own research investigations. Renzulli believes that all students should be given the opportunity to develop higher order thinking skills and pursue enriched high-end learning.

When implementing the Enrichment Triad Model in the classroom, the teacher's priority is the development of independence and encouragement of self-directed learning. The open endedness of this model gives students the freedom to make choices about topics, resources, and manner of presentation. Teachers will also find a freedom in structure that allows them to guide their students through investigations and projects step by step, while still being able to change the process to suit the needs of individual students.

The Three Types of Activities

There are three types of activities within the Triad Model. They are the following:

Type I — Exploratory Experiences
Students' interests are identified. Students are given the opportunity to explore something new and extend their learning within a familiar topic.

Type II — Group Training Activities
These activities promote the development of thinking and feeling processes with a major focus on advanced levels of thinking. These activities provide students with the necessary skills to carry out individual and small group investigations and include the following:

- creative and critical thinking skills
- decision making
- problem solving
- communication skills, and
- research skills.

These activities develop "learning how to learn" skills. They focus on:

- becoming more creative
- research techniques, and
- how to use different types of equipment.

Type III — Individual and/or Small Group Investigations of Real Issues
Students use appropriate methods of research and inquiry to develop management plans to aid in completion of the investigation.

Type I and II enrichment activities provide the basic skills needed for students to carry out their own or group investigations. Type III enrichment activities require a high level of commitment from the students and actively engage them in the learning process by expecting them to add new knowledge, ideas, or products to a field of study. (**Note**: Ensure that students have participated in Type I and Type II activities before embarking on a Type III activity.)

All three types of enrichment activities are interrelated to a high degree within the model. The diagram below illustrates this interrelation.

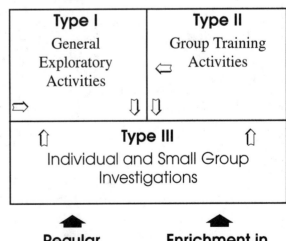

Overview for the
Classroom Teacher

Classroom Management

The Enrichment Triad Model emphasizes high quality outcomes for students that reflect the amount of understanding and the depth of thought of participating students. Depending upon ability in relation to the task at hand, students may start at any point within the model; however, allowing students to embark on Type III activities without background knowledge and training (Type I and II activities) may result in a poor or less than worthwhile investigation.

Type I

Students need to be given freedom to explore a variety of topics. This exploration must be purposeful and students must come up with some ideas for what they would like to study and how they will go about this.

For example: A student may be interested in insects. The student then looks at material related to insects and develops questions to be investigated. These may include the following:

- Why do insects only have six legs?

- Do all insects have the same body structure?

- What does an insect do?

The student will also come up with a plan to find the information to answer these questions. For example the student might:

- interview the curator at a local museum

- find and observe insects in their natural habitat.

Teachers need to help students identify areas of study and stimulate their interest. To start the process, ask students to talk about their interests. Once a student has identified an area of interest, the teacher needs to keep checking on progress by holding formal and informal meetings to discuss findings.

Type I activities should assist the teacher to decide which Type II activities need to be taught to particular groups of students.

Type II

As these activities are training exercises to help the student deal more effectively with finding content, the teacher must ensure that the skills are first taught in a content-free lesson. Once the skills are internalized, the student can apply them to a specific task.

These skills focus on critical analysis, problem solving, and divergent and creative thinking.

Type III

Not all students pursue an individual or small group investigation for every topic. Type III enrichment activities are designed to do the following:

- foster a desire to find out more about a topic of interest

- provide an opportunity for those students who have shown interest, willingness, and commitment to carry out an investigation of their own

- actively engage students in the formulation of a real issue and decision about a plan of action, and

- encourage students to produce new information for their topic and to present their findings to audiences for whom there is some relevance.

Renzulli's Enrichment Triad for English

General

- Create learning centers that cater to diverse interests and learning styles.
- Involve mentors or peer tutors.
- Encourage students to participate fully in Type II activities.
- Ensure that students' communication skills (speaking, writing, listening, and reading) are developed efficiently through activities that are exciting and relevant.

Type I

- Hold a class brainstorming session to identify areas of interest or themes. Compile a list of these and vote for the most popular. Ask students to think of topics they wish to pursue within the chosen theme.
- Invite guest speakers to talk to students about different topics related to the theme.
- Create interest centers related to the theme under study. Include items to provoke curiosity rather than simply present information. Encourage students to create these centers. More than one interest center can be created simultaneously.
- Divide the class into the number of interest centers and over a number of days, allow students to explore each one.
- Field trips to relevant venues are ideal for this exploratory phase. If possible link the field trip to the popular interest centers.

Type II

- Devise simple research projects to develop the research skills of locating, recording, and reporting information. For example:
  - Volume research: Find out all you can about one of the planets in our solar system.
  - Focused research: Choose a famous person and find out why that person is famous.
  - Explanatory research: Find out why dinosaurs are no longer on Earth.
- Ask students to devise questions for surveys that will involve gathering and interpreting information. For example,
  - How many of our class have red cars, blue eyes, cats?
  - How do we get to school?
- Ask students to think creatively about solutions to different problems. For example,
  - What can we do with all of the hair that people have cut off each year?
  - How could we recycle daily rubbish?'
- Assist students to develop questioning skills: For example,
  - Having listened to a story, students write two questions about each character, if they can.
  - Show students an unfamiliar object and ask them to think of some questions that will help them establish what the object is.
  - Give students the answers to a list of questions and ask them to suggest the questions that have given rise to these. For example, A: I do not like Brussel sprouts./Q: What is your least favorite vegetable? What is your least favorite food? What is one vegetable you don't like?

Type III

- Assist students in developing their investigation plans consisting of three parts:
  - Aim: What they want to find out?
  - Method: How they are going to find it out?
  - Report: How they will present their findings (to the teacher or class)?
- Set aside regular times when students can meet with their mentors to discuss progress.
- Provide time for students to present their investigations to their peers or invited guests.

Name:

Type I–Interest Identification

1 Draw four things you would like to find out more about.

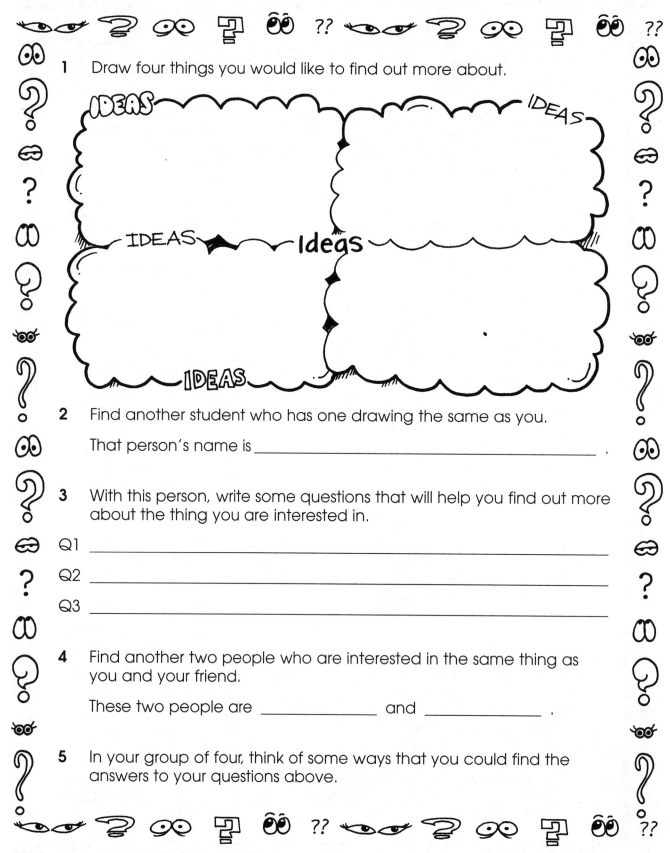

IDEAS   IDEAS

IDEAS   Ideas

IDEAS

2 Find another student who has one drawing the same as you.

That person's name is _____ .

3 With this person, write some questions that will help you find out more about the thing you are interested in.

Q1 _____

Q2 _____

Q3 _____

4 Find another two people who are interested in the same thing as you and your friend.

These two people are _____ and _____ .

5 In your group of four, think of some ways that you could find the answers to your questions above.

Name:

Management
Strategies:

★ ■ ▼

RENZULLI'S
TRIAD

English

BLM 24

Type II—Creative Thinking Skills, Originality

Airplanes

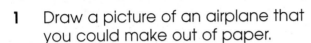

1 Draw a picture of an airplane that you could make out of paper.

2 Make this airplane and fly it.

3 Draw what happened when you flew your airplane.

4 What could you do to make your airplane better?

I could _____

_____

_____

_____

_____

5 Make a new airplane, using these changes and see what happens.

6 Draw what happened.

7 What else could you do to make your airplane fly further and higher?

I could _____

_____

_____

_____

_____

8 Find some friends and fly your airplanes in a contest to see whose is the best.

Renzulli's Enrichment Triad for Math

General

- For more able students, use individual contracts and guidelines for the completion of work.
- Collect hands-on resources so that students can explore concepts while manipulating material in real-life situations.
- Involve students in games that require the application of problem solving skills such as dominoes, UNO, tic tac toe and Chinese checkers.
- Use skill centers that help students apply and extend particular skills (numeration, patterning, problem solving, money) in real-life situations.

Type I

- Create opportunities for students to explore properties of number using hands-on materials. For example,
  - Arrange 15 counters in as many different ways as they can, using addition, multiplication, place value, and writing the corresponding number sentences.
- Ask students to match mathematical terms with cards that show that term being applied. For example,
  - addition 15 +7
  - time 7:30 p.m.
  - shape triangle
- Ask students to brainstorm all the things they do during the day that involve math.

Type II

- Conduct surveys in which students collect, record, and interpret data. For example,
  - Interview the class about which pets they have at home.

- Follow up with evaluative questions.
  - What is the third most popular pet? If you owned a pet shop which four animals would sell best?
- Create opportunities for students to make and check predictions. For example,
  - Which object will weigh more?
  - Which object is longer/shorter?
  - Which group of counters has more in it?
  - Which bundle of blocks is even?
- Provide problems for students to solve. For example:
  - A farmer has 12 sheep and 15 cows. How many animals does the farmer have altogether?
  - If a school has 12 classes and there are 25 students in each class, how many students are there altogether?
  - How many different ways can you express the number 285?
- Encourage students to complete small research projects. For example,
  - How have numbers been written down in the past?
  - What ways do we measure time?
  - When would a cook use math?

Type III

- Ask students to write a plan of action prior to starting their investigation.
- Ask students how they will present their findings and who their audience will be.
- Ask students to explain how they carried out their investigation and the methods they used.

Name:

Type II—Research
Sundials

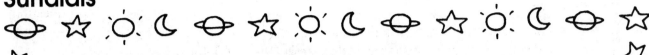

 1 Draw some instruments that have been used to measure time.

2 Draw a sundial below and describe what it will be made from.

My sundial will look like this:

My sundial will be made from this:

_____

_____

_____

_____

_____

3 Explain how sundials work.

_____

_____

_____

4 Where would be the best place on the playground to put your sundial?

_____

5 On the back of this sheet, illustrate what your sundial will look like on the playground.

Name:

Management
Strategies:

Type II—Group Research
Television Habits

People in our group:

_____

Conduct a survey to find out of the following information:

How many hours
of TV do your
friends watch
each day?

What are their
favorite
programs?

What shows do
they not like to
watch?

Questions our group will ask:

1. _____   2. _____

3. _____   4. _____

On the back of this sheet, draw up a table to record the answers.

Show your results the following ways:

Picture graph	Bar graph	Your choice

Renzulli's Enrichment Triad for Science

General

- Create learning centers related to themes across curriculum areas that reflect the interests of the students. For example, dinosaur evolution, ecology, looking at insects and bugs, astronomy with a focus on the planets and stars.

- Encourage students to question what they see in terms of how or why something happened.

- Encourage students' natural curiosity by presentations that show an end result rather than simply giving information about the topic; for example, construct a volcano that actually explodes.

- Assist students to look at a problem from many different angles and come up with more than one solution.

Type I

- Visit the local science center where students can have hands-on experience in all facets of science.

- Allow students to carry out simple experiments under adult supervision.

- Have an "animal day" where students bring in pets and visitors bring in unusual animals.

- Make available pictures and books on a variety of different topics related to a theme or students' interests.

Type II

- Promote discussion among students of solutions to problems. For example,

  - How could Jack and Jill have taken the water down the hill without carrying a heavy bucket?

  - What would we do if there were no telephones?

  - How could we help people get better if antibiotics had not been invented?

- Ask students to chart the weather over a period of time. Encourage them to make some assumptions about the weather and the season. For example, "It is getting colder because it is now winter."

- Ask students to complete small-scale investigations. Let them discuss ways to investigate these questions and how they will present their findings. For example:

  - What type of food do we eat during the day?

  - Is it good for us or not?

- Allow students to complete research projects that will help them identify ways to gather information and record and summarize data. For example:

  - What does the moon look like?

  - How do fish swim?

  - How do plants grow?

Type III

- Ask students to plan how their investigation will take place and the methods they will use to solve their hypothesis or meet the goals they have identified.

- Ask students what the relevance of their investigation is to them personally.

- Hold a science fair so that students can present their findings to a variety of people.

Name:

Type II–Small Scale Investigation
Food Diary

1 Keep a diary for one week of what you eat before and at school.

Monday	Tuesday	Wednesday	Thursday	Friday
Morning	Morning	Morning	Morning	Morning
Lunch	Lunch	Lunch	Lunch	Lunch

2 Sort these into the five food groups below.

Fats	Cereals & Bread	Meat & Fish	Carbohydrates	Fruit & Vegetables

3 Which group has the most foods in it?

_____

4 Compare your diary and chart to those of your friends.

5 On a separate piece of paper, make a graph to show how much from each food group is eaten by you and your friends in one week. Write three statements about the information in your graph.

Name:

Management
Strategies:

◗ ♣

RENZULLI'S
TRIAD
Science
BLM 28

Type I–Predictions and Checking
Visit to the Supermarket

Before you go:

1   On the back of this sheet, draw four different jobs you think you'll see being done at the supermarket.

2   Write down some food items you think you'll see in these food sections.

Dairy Section	Meat Section	Bakery	Fruit & Veggies	Frozen Foods

After you have visited the supermarket:

3   Draw four jobs that you saw people doing at the supermarket.

4   Write down some food items you actually found in these food sections.

Dairy Section	Meat Section	Bakery	Fruit & Veggies	Frozen Foods

5   Did your predictions match with what you actually saw at the supermarket? _____

_____

Thinking Caps

Notes and Activities

by Fay Holbert

Overview for the Classroom Teacher

Introduction to Thinking Caps

The thinking caps are inspired by Dr. de Bono's concepts in teaching thinking skills. They provide a means whereby students can identify and utilize all their thinking processes when faced with an issue. They also help students to discuss their thinking processes.

Each cap represents a different thinking approach:

Cap	Uses	Purpose	Questions to ask
Feelings Cap	• Making feelings known • Assessments and choices	• Alternatives • Emotions, feelings • Hunches, intuition	Which one do I like best? How do I feel about this?
Positive Cap	• Good points • Benefits • Why it will work • Likelihood	• Assessing and valuing • Extracting benefits • Making something work	Why is this worth doing? How will it help us? Why can it be done? Why will it help us?
Negative Cap	• Check for evidence • Check for logic • Feasibility • Impact • Weaknesses	• Find weaknesses • Makes assessments	Is this true? Will it work? What are the weaknesses? What is wrong with it?
Creative Cap	• Generate reactive ideas • Start ideas • Further, better, new ideas	• Creativity • Gives possibilities and alternatives	What are some ways to work this out /solve the problem? What ideas do we have?
Research Cap	• Identify what is relevant /most important/valid • Identify the information we have/need • Identify how to get the information we need	• Stimulate thinking • Check thinking	What information do we have? What information do we need to get?
Planning Cap	• Define focus/purpose • Set out thinking plan or agenda • Make observations and comments • Decide on the next step • Define outcomes • Summarise	• Be constructive • Thinking about thinking	What have we done so far? What do we do next? What is the next step? (often whole group)

* These students appear on the BLMs and task cards following to indicate some thinking strategies.

Overview for the Classroom Teacher

THINKING CAPS NOTES

How Do the Caps Work?

The different caps allow students to approach an issue from six different points of view. Instead of trying to do everything at once, students learn to handle the different aspects of thinking one at a time. Finally, different aspects come together to give wide-range thinking.

Our egos are very involved in our thinking. We get attached to an argument or an idea and find it difficult to stand back and be objective. The role-playing in the thinking caps helps students to detach the ego from the thinking – "This is not me, but my positive cap speaking". With the thinking caps, if we don't like a suggestion, we know that there will always be a chance to criticize it with the negative cap and to express feelings with the feelings cap. Meanwhile, it is possible to explore the idea with the research, positive, and creative caps.

It is very important that every thinker is able to switch roles: put caps on and take caps off. The purpose and value of the thinking caps is to get students to use all six modes of thinking.

Beware: Students tend to overuse the negative cap. Students tend to under-use the creative cap. When using the planning cap, be careful not to interrupt the line of thinking.

Four Styles for the Teacher to Use:

1.   Put the cap on.
Address one student or a whole group:
"Give me some negative cap thinking."
"We're stuck. Can you put on your creative cap?"

2.   Take the cap off.
Move away from a particular line of thinking:
"That's feeling cap thinking. Can you take off your feeling cap?"
"You've thought of lots of new ideas, but I think we should take off our creative caps now."

3.   Switch caps.
This way teachers can call for a switch in thinking without hurting the student's feelings. We are not attacking the thinking but asking for a change:
"We've heard the good things. Let's switch from the positive cap to the negative cap. What problems might there be if we do it like that?"

4.   Signal your thinking.
Use the caps yourself and point out that you are using them as you teach the class.

Thinking Cap Sequences

The thinking caps are repeatedly used in sequence when students are confronted by more complicated thinking tasks. After a practice session, invite your students to recall the sequences they used. These observations provide a good basis for further discussions about the ways we approach thinking about problems and finding resolutions. Some common sequences follow:

First Ideas: Planning — Research — Creative

Quick Assessment: Positive ——Planning

Evaluation: Positive ——Negative

Improvement: Negative ——Creative

Explanation: Research — Creative

Direct Action: Feelings — Negative

Emotions: Feelings ——Research ——Creative — Planning

Caution: Research — Negative

Opportunity: Research — Positive

Design: Planning — Creative ——Feelings

Possibilities: Creative ——Planning

Useable Alternatives: Creative — Positive — Negative

Choice: Positive — Negative — Feelings

Final Assessment: Negative — Feelings

Thinking Caps in English

Theme: Toys and Games

Following are some thinking strategies for the theme of toys and games. Ask students to approach each question wearing the nominated caps. For example, in "Choices", ask them to put on their feelings caps first and brainstorm which of the games they liked the best. When you have your list, ask students to put on their positive caps and list the good points for each of these games, etc.

First Thoughts

- Display a collection of the students' favorite toys and games. Ask the class to question each owner about his or her game. For example:

  - Where did you get this game? (Research)

  - Was it very expensive? (Research)

  - How does it work? What does it do? What do you have to do? What are the rules? (Research)

  - Why do you like it? (Feelings)

  - Why do you like it better than other games? (Feelings, Positive)

Choices

- After all the students have seen how all the toys work and the games are played, ask each student to decide which three he or she would like to own. Record the selections as preparation for a brainstorming session. (Feelings, Positive, Negative)

  - What sort of games do you like best? (Feelings)

  - What do you like about these games? (Positive)

  - What sorts of games don't you like? (Negative)

Evaluation

- Are there any obvious similarities between the choices of the boys and those of the girls? (Planning)

- Should there be games for boys and games for girls? Why? (Positive, Negative, Feelings)

- Are there any games or toys that you can think of that would be unsuitable for some children? Why do you think this? (Negative, Feelings)

Improvement

- Could you improve any of these games/toys so they would be suitable for all children? How? (Creative)

Speculation

- If you could have any game or toy you wanted (not only those on display), what would you have to consider before you chose? (Planning, Feelings, Positive)

- If all your toys were locked away for a week, could you design your own game to play?

  - What would you have to consider? (Planning)

  - How would you go about it? (Creative)

- Do you think that all games should be designed so there is always a winner? (Planning, Feelings)

- Name some games that do not result in winners or losers. (Research, Planning)

Name:

Management Strategies:

Toys and Games

1 Make a list of five toys and games you have or would like to have. Complete the following table.

Toy/Game (RESEARCH)	Good Points (POSITIVE)	Bad Points (NEGATIVE)	Score /10 (FEELINGS)
1.			
2.			
3.			
4.			
5.			

2 Consider the game of marbles. List what you have to do to play a game of marbles and enjoy it.

3 List how you could change the game so it can be played by the following students:

Is In a wheelchair	Cannot see	Cannot hear

Thinking Caps in English

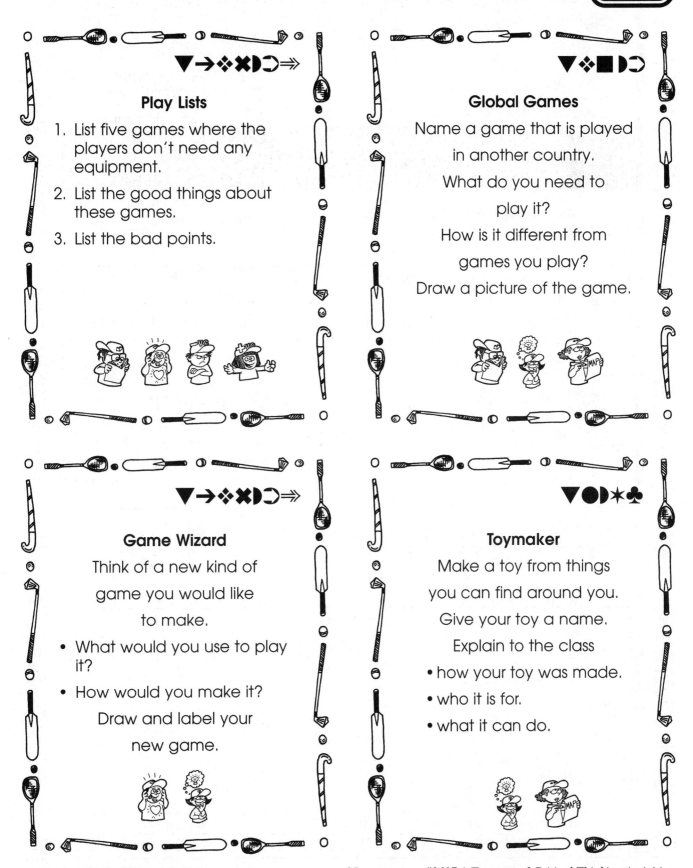

Play Lists

1. List five games where the players don't need any equipment.
2. List the good things about these games.
3. List the bad points.

Global Games

Name a game that is played in another country.

What do you need to play it?

How is it different from games you play?

Draw a picture of the game.

Game Wizard

Think of a new kind of game you would like to make.

- What would you use to play it?
- How would you make it?
  Draw and label your new game.

Toymaker

Make a toy from things you can find around you.

Give your toy a name.

Explain to the class

- how your toy was made.
- who it is for.
- what it can do.

Thinking Caps in Math

Theme: Weight

Arrange a display of

- different types of scales

- several items such as grocery goods that have weights indicated on them.

First Thoughts

Ask students the following:

- What do we use to measure weight? (Research)

- What are the names of some measurements we use when weighing objects? (Research)

- How much do you weigh? Ask all students to check their weights on available scales. (Research)

Assessing

Discuss with students the following questions:

- Name some things we buy by weight. Why do you think we buy these things in this way? (Research, Positive, Creative)

- Which items do you know of that are bought by kilograms (kg) or grams (g)? Why do we have different measurements like these? (Research, Positive, Negative)

- Which other measurements are used for weighing things? Why do we need more than kilograms and grams? (Research, Creative)

Prediction and Checking

Ask students to predict and verify the following:

- Which would weigh more, this book or this pencil case? Check estimation. (Planning, Feelings)

- How many pencils would I need to weigh the same as this apple? Check estimation. (Planning, Feelings)

- Who would weigh about the same as you (or a friend)? Check. (Positive, Negative, Feelings)

- Place a stone on some balance scales. Find some items to balance the weight of the stone. Write your equation. (Creative, Positive, Negative)

Stimulate Thinking

Involve students in the following problems:

- Weigh some grocery items to check the weights. Why is there a difference between what the label says and the actual weight of the can/packet, etc? (Research, Creative)

- What is meant by the term "standard weights"? In what ways are standard measurements important for everyone? (All Caps)

Thinking Caps in Math

▼→◧✹◆⇒♣

Scaling Scales

Draw as many different types of scales as you can. Invent your own weighing machine that can show what is heavier, lighter, or equal in weight. Draw and label your scales.

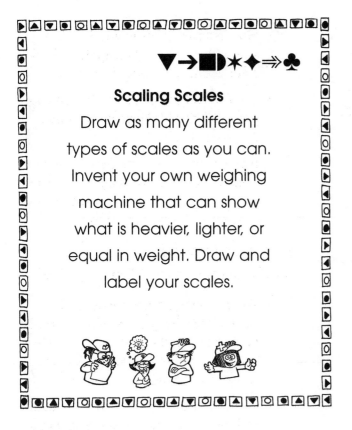

▼→◧✹◆⇒♣

Let's Talk About Weight!

Select any five items from your classroom. Without weighing them, put them in order from heaviest to lightest.
Check your guess by weighing the items.

▼◗✹❖

Measuring Up

Find out which countries use a different way of measuring from ours. What do they use? Compare the different ways of measuring.

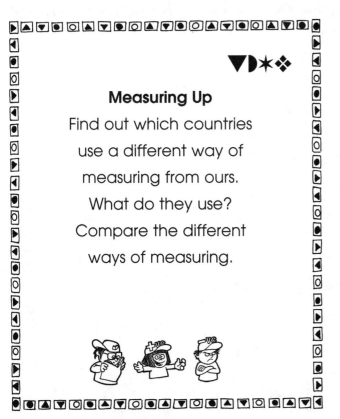

▼◧✹◆⇒♣

Heavy Questions

Think of a new way to price grocery store produce.
What are the good and bad points of your new method?
Is it fair for everyone?

Name:

Standard Measurements

Management Strategies:

▼ → ❖ ■ ◗

★ ◆ ✛ ⇒

1   List the standard measurements you know.

_____

_____

_____

_____

2   Write down some reasons why we need standard measurements.

_____

_____

3   What do you think traders used before there were standard weights?

_____

_____

4   Write down some difficulties using non-standard measurement.

_____

_____

5   You have a 2 kg and a 3 kg weight.

How will you measure out the following amounts of bananas?

(There may be more than one way.)

     7 kg   **10 kg**   **1 kg**   **20 kg**

All About Scales

1 Do all scales show us weight only? If not, what else could they show? Draw your answers here:

2 Write down four reasons why scales that show extra information are useful.

_____   _____

_____   _____

3 Who would find these scales useful? Write down at least three ideas.

_____   _____

_____

4 On the back of the page, draw a picture of someone using some scales.

Thinking Caps in Health

Theme: Movement

First Thoughts

- Brainstorm: "What are ways that creatures can move?" Record all answers, showing the types of movements and the animals who perform the movement. For example:

  - fly — birds

  - walk — humans. (Research)

- Ask this question: "Do all animals move?'" (Planning, Research)

- Ask students to think about the many creatures that can move in more than one fashion; for example, humans can walk, run, hop, climb, swim, etc. Now ask students to name creatures that move in only one way. (Research, Planning)

Possibilities and Impossibilities

- Returning to your original brainstorming information, discuss "Which body parts do creatures use to perform their movements?" (Research, Positive, Negative)

- Now ask students to consider some impossibilities. Ask them to think about why it would be impossible for

  - a sheep to swim

  - a rhinoceros to fly

  - a fish to run

  - an earthworm to run? (Creative, Research, Planning, Negative)

Evaluation/Explanation

- How important is a creature's habitat in deciding the manner in which it moves? Think of creatures that live in jungles, deserts, mountains, and water.

  - How and why does habitat have an effect? (Planning, Positive, Feelings)

- Following on from this, consider why survival would be impossible for

  - a fish in a forest

  - a snake in Antarctica

  - a penguin in the mountains

  - a walrus in the desert? (Negative, Planning, Creative)

- Discuss with students why some animals move quickly and some move very slowly. What do they notice about all of the fast movers? (Research, Creative, Planning)

- Ask students to list how animals' bodies have developed their bodies to be able to obtain the best movement. (Planning, Research, Positive)

Prediction, Possibilities

- How would you cope with being a different animal?

  - Divide the class into small groups (5 or 6). Take the students onto the playground. Ask them to try to imitate the movements of other animals. Use the monkey bars, sandpit, balance beams, stepping stones, flat areas, steep areas, etc. (Creative, Planning, Positive, Negative)

Management Strategies:

▼ →
● ⊃

THINKING CAPS

Health

BLM 32

Movement

1. Write down four reasons why animals need to move.

    1. _____   3. _____

    2. _____   4. _____

2. Choose three animals and fill in the table to show some of the different ways each one moves.

Animal	Method 1	Method 2	Method 3

3. Of your three animals, draw the fast movers on the left and the slow movers on the right.

Fast Movers	Slow Movers

4. Invent a creature that would be the best mover ever. On the back of this paper, draw and label your "pet" to show the special purposes for the special parts.

Name:

Talking About Birds

1. Ducks, geese, turkeys, and chickens are all domestic birds called fowls. They can all fly a bit but some fly better than others.

In the table below rank these birds from worst to best flyers:

Worst Flyer	Bad Flyer	Better	Best

2. Why are ducks and geese able to swim but turkeys and chickens are not?

   Illustrate your answer.

Make Your Own Task Cards

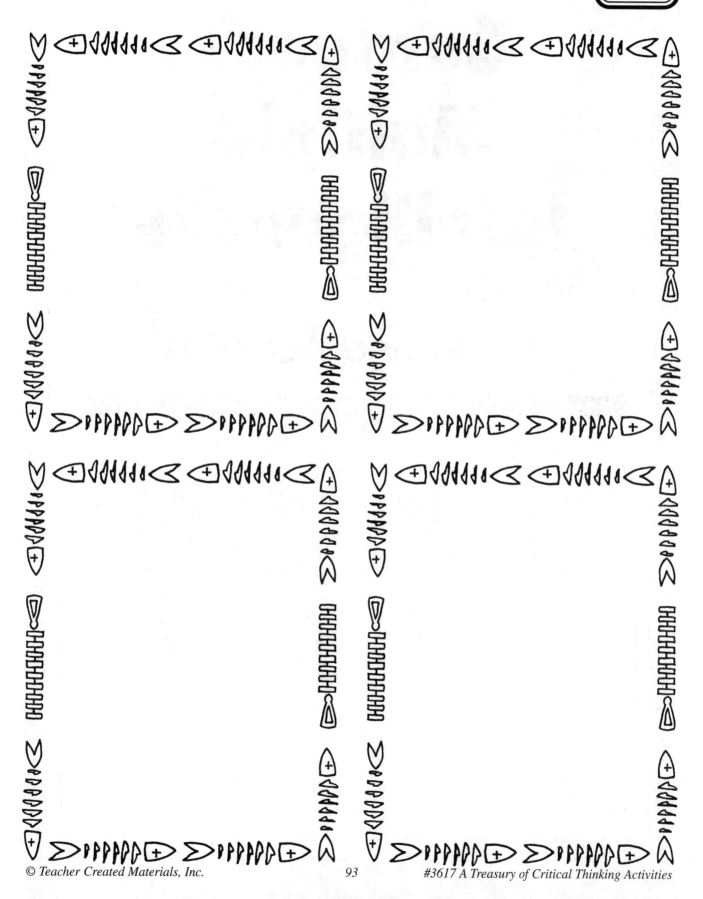

Gardner's Multiple Intelligences

Notes and Activities

by Fay Holbert

Overview for the Classroom Teacher

GARDNER'S MULTIPLE INTELLIGENCES
NOTES

Introduction to Howard Gardner's 'Multiple Intelligences'

Gardner defines intelligence as "the ability to solve problems, or to create products, that are valued within one or more cultural setting/s." He maintains that it should be possible to identify an individual's educational profile at an early age, and then draw upon this knowledge to enhance that person's educational opportunities and options. An educator should be able to channel individuals with unusual talents into special enrichment programs. To this end, he has developed a framework, building on the theory of multiple intelligences, that can be applied to any educational situation.

Because of Gardner's work, many educators believe that education is not merely a means to sort out a few children and make them leaders, but to develop the latent talents of the entire population in diverse ways.

If we are to understand our children's potential, we must take into consideration all of their abilities and not just those that can be tested with standardized instruments such as an I.Q. test. What is important in educational terms is not which intelligences we are strongest in, but our own particular blend of strengths and weaknesses.

The importance attached to the I.Q., however, is not entirely inappropriate – the score does predict a person's ability to achieve in school subjects. Its limitation is that it predicts little of the successes in later life.

So, what of the wider range of performances that are valued in different parts of the world? For example: a 12 year old boy from the Caroline Islands who has shown some ability is selected by his elders to learn how to become a master sailor and undertake study of navigation, geography and the stars; and a 15 year old Iranian youth who has committed to heart the entire Koran and mastered the Arabic language will train to be a teacher and religious leader.

It is obvious that these two young people

are displaying intelligent behavior, and it is equally clear that the present method of assessing intellect is not going to allow an accurate assessment of their potential or their achievements. Only if we expand and rethink our views of what counts as human intellect will we, as educators, be able to devise more appropriate ways of assessing it, and more effective ways of educating it.

Gardner's "Intelligences" are:

- Verbal/Linguistic
- Logical/Mathematical
- Visual/Spatial
- Bodily/Kinesthetic
- Musical/Rhythmical
- Interpersonal
- Intrapersonal

Recently Gardner has added a new intelligence: Nature/Environmental

Learning Centers

The classroom teacher should give equal time and attention to each intelligence every day. One way to achieve this is to maintain various learning centers in the classroom, one for each of the intelligences.

A Note About This Section

Pages 98–104 of this section look at one theme from the perspective of the various "intelligences." The rest of the pages include activities for all the intelligences in the four main curriculum areas.

Overview for the Classroom Teacher

Details and Description of Gardner's Multiple Intelligences

Verbal/Linguistic (V/L)

This student enjoys words—reading, writing, storytelling, humor/jokes. He/she participates eagerly in debates, story/poetry writing, journal/diary keeping and has a sensitivity to language.

- *writer, poet, novelist, journalist, psycho-linguist (L/M), signing*

Logical/Mathematical (L/M)

This student loves numbers, patterns, relationships, formulas. He/she shines at mathematics, reasoning, logic, problem solving, and deciphering codes and enjoys pattern games, calculation, number sequences, outlining.

- *scientist, mathematician, engineer, technician*

Visual/Spatial (V/S)

This student loves drawing, building, designing, creating, visualizing colors, pictures, observing, patterns/designs. He/she enjoys creating models, mind mapping, pretending and has an active imagination.

- *artist, cartographer, navigator, decorator, chess player*

Bodily/Kinesthetic (B/K)

This student has to touch, move, handle objects. He/she enjoys dance, drama, role-play, mime, sports games, physical gestures, martial arts and is great with body control, refining movement, expression through movement, inventing, interaction.

- *athlete, surgeon (L/M), dancer/choreographer (M/R)*

Musical/Rhythmical (M/R)

This student loves sounds, melody, rhythm, playing instruments, singing, vocal sounds/tones. He/she needs to be involved with music composition/creation, and music performances and enjoys percussion, humming, environmental/instrumental sounds, tonal and rhythmic patterns.

- *musician, composer, sound engineer (L/M), music critic (V/L)*

Interpersonal (Ier)

The student who likes interacting, talking, giving and receiving feedback, group projects, cooperative learning strategies, division of labor. He/she needs to be involved in collaborative tasks and person to person communication. This student is always intuitive to others' feelings and motives and is empathetic.

- *Administrator, coach, mental health, physician (L/M), teacher (various).*

Intrapersonal (Ira)

This student wants to work alone, pursue personal interests, understands self, and has introspective feelings and dreams. He/she displays silent reflective methods, higher order reasoning and metacognition techniques, emotional processing, focus/concentration skills, and complex guided imagery, "centering" practices.

- *writer (V/L), inventor (L/M)*

Nature/Environmental (N/E)

Recently, Gardner has included an eighth intelligence which he calls "Nature/Environmental." Not a lot of information is yet available from Gardner on this intelligence, but it is summarized as one involving the recognition and classification of species in the environment and how we can best preserve this environment for the greatest benefit to all.

- *veterinarian, zoologist, botanist, national park ranger, landscape gardener (V/L), florist*

Note: The "students" described here appear on the task cards and BLMs that follow to indicate the "intelligence" to which that activity is primarily targeted.

Gardner's Multiple Intelligences Activities

Theme: Land Transportation

Many of the activities that follow are not exclusive to one intelligence, but may involve two or more. For example, those asking for illustrations involve Visual/Spatia, and those requiring oral and/or written presentations involve Verbal/Linguistic, etc.

Where questions could be answered with a "yes" or "no" response, probe further.

Verbal/Linguistic

- What do we mean by "transportation"? Build up a vocabulary for land transportation — pre-wheel to modern day.
- Which animals might have been used to assist with transportation?
- What forms of transportation do you use? Compare your responses with those of your classmates.

Logical/Mathematical

- Time how long it takes to walk to school.
- How does this time compare with riding or being driven to school? Explain.
- Is your time the same as/similar to your classmates' times? Explain.
- How far do you live from the school/shopping center?

Visual/Spatial

- Do cars look the same now as they did 10, 20, 50 years ago? How are they different/the same?
- Has the way people travel changed much over the last 100, 200, 500 years? How?
- Design a type of land transportation that would be suitable for young people to use to go to school or do the family shopping.

Bodily/Kinesthetic

- Which sports involve using types of transportation? What types are used?
- What is the same about all the contests that involve types of transportation?

Explain.
- How could you improve the vehicles used?
- Why are there different types of transportation?

Musical/Rhythmical

- What "travel songs" do you know?
- Ask the class to guess how you are travelling when you
  - mime different rhythms of transportation.
  - create sounds of travel/transportation.

Interpersonal

- How is transportation useful?
- How is transportation a danger?
- What are we doing to try to make transportation less dangerous?
- Why don't these ideas always work?

Intrapersonal

- If you had to travel a short distance (a kilometer or less), how would you travel?
- If you had to travel a long way (thousands of kilometers), how would you travel?
- If you could travel anywhere at all: where would you go; when would you go; how long would you stay; and how would you get there?
- If you lived 100 years ago, how would you have preferred to travel about?
- What type of transportation would you like to own now? Why?

Nature/Environmental

- If you couldn't ask anyone and you wanted to find out about transportation in a certain community, how would you go about it? You want to know if there is transportation, what type there is, and where to find it.
- Does transportation damage the environment? How?
- How could this change be reduced or ended?

Activities for Land Transportation

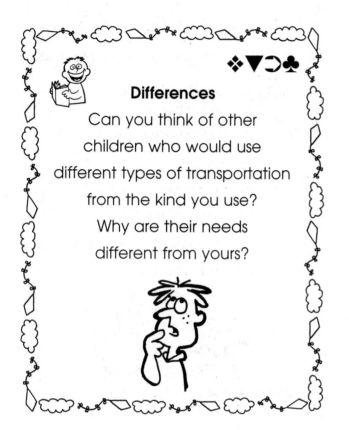

Differences

Can you think of other children who would use different types of transportation from the kind you use? Why are their needs different from yours?

Cycle Safety

Make a list of the safety equipment that all bicycles and cyclists should have.

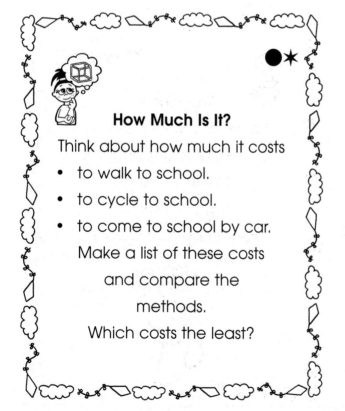

How Much Is It?

Think about how much it costs

- to walk to school.
- to cycle to school.
- to come to school by car.

Make a list of these costs and compare the methods.
Which costs the least?

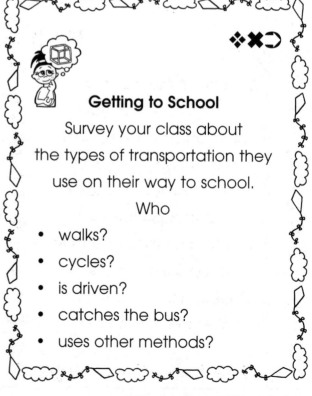

Getting to School

Survey your class about the types of transportation they use on their way to school.

Who

- walks?
- cycles?
- is driven?
- catches the bus?
- uses other methods?

Activities for Land Transportation

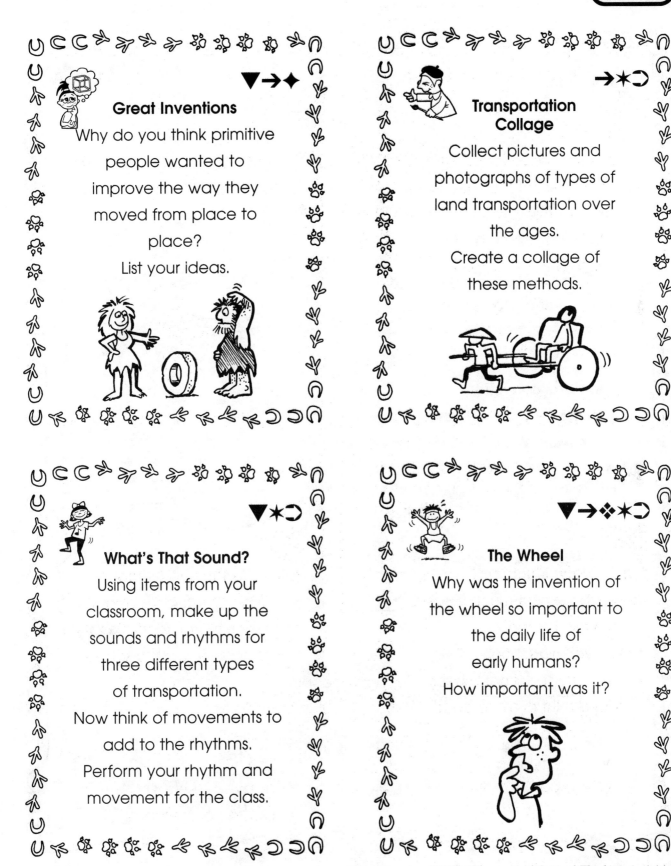

Great Inventions

▼→◆

Why do you think primitive people wanted to improve the way they moved from place to place?
List your ideas.

Transportation Collage

→✳◖

Collect pictures and photographs of types of land transportation over the ages.
Create a collage of these methods.

What's That Sound?

▼✳◖

Using items from your classroom, make up the sounds and rhythms for three different types of transportation.
Now think of movements to add to the rhythms.
Perform your rhythm and movement for the class.

The Wheel

▼→◆✳◖

Why was the invention of the wheel so important to the daily life of early humans?
How important was it?

Activities for Land Transportation

GARDNER'S
MULTIPLE
INTELLIGENCES
TASK CARDS

Comparisons

What are the advantages and disadvantages of these types of transportation?

Walking

Taking a taxi

Riding a horse

Riding a tractor

Cycling

Using a skateboard

Catching a bus

Taking a train

Skiing

Riding a motor bike

Remote Transportation

Imagine that you live in these places:

Sahara, Antarctica, the jungle, Andes

Draw pictures of how you would travel there. There may be more than one way to travel in some areas.

Moving Goods

Transportation is not just used to move people around. It is also used to move goods from place to place.

List the good things and bad things about these ways of carrying goods:

wagon   truck   train.

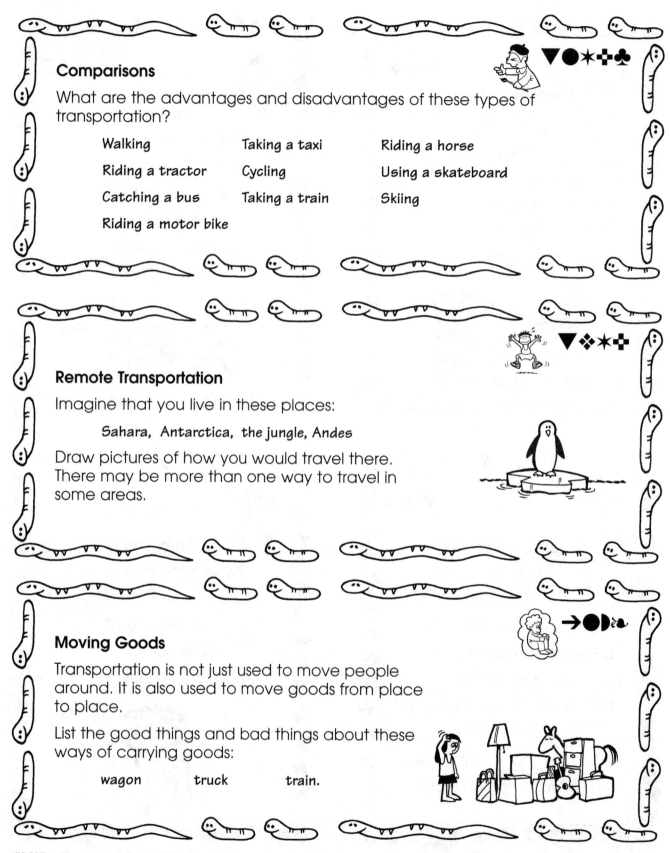

Activities for Land Transportation

GARDNER'S MULTIPLE INTELLIGENCES

TASK CARDS

Earlier Days

Ask your grandparents or elderly friends about the land transportation they used when they were your age.

Ask someone from another country about the transportation there.

Draw pictures of the types of transportation you find out about.

Animals and Transportation

Make a list of the animals which were used in the past to transport things.

Which animals are still used in this way?

Collect pictures and photographs of these animals at work.

Special Vehicles

Have you ever seen types of transportation that have been changed to help people who have a disability?

Explain to your class

- what you have seen, and

- how the changes help.

Name:

Environment Watch

1. What kind of damage has been done to the environment by modern methods of transportation?

   Make a list here: _____

   _____

   _____

2. Draw a picture of some of the damage that has been caused by the various types of transportation.

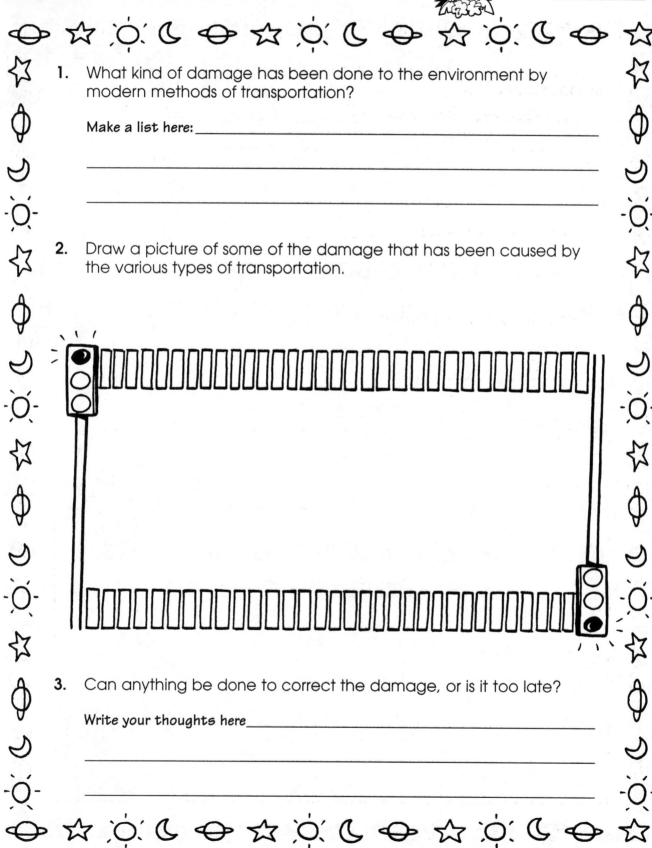

3. Can anything be done to correct the damage, or is it too late?

   Write your thoughts here_____

   _____

   _____

Name: _____

My Favorite Transportation

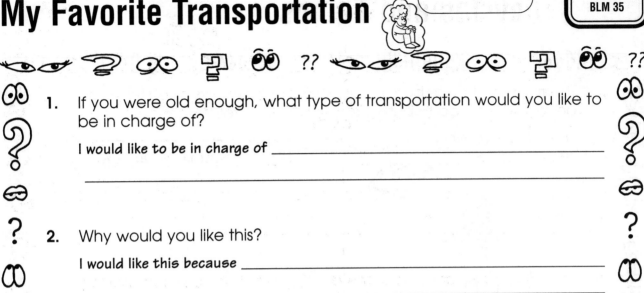

1. If you were old enough, what type of transportation would you like to be in charge of?

   I would like to be in charge of _____

   _____

2. Why would you like this?

   I would like this because _____

   _____

3. What would you do with it?

   I would _____

   _____

4. Draw a picture of yourself using this type of transportation.

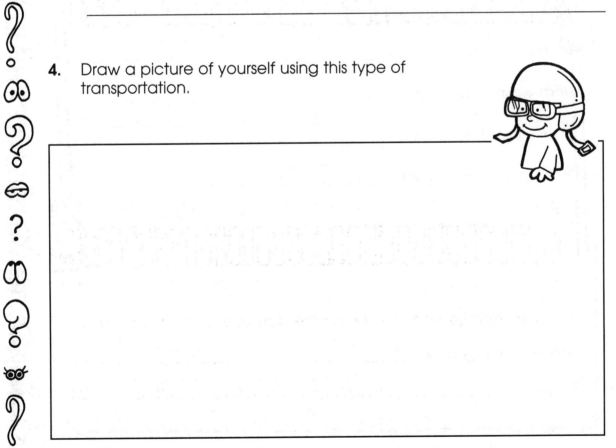

Name:

Bicycles and Things

1. The first bicycle was built in England over 360 years ago. It had no pedals. Riders had to push it along with their feet!

   Draw this invention.

   Bicycle from the year 1642

2. Now think about a futuristic "personal transportation machine."

   How would it move? _____

   What would it be made of? _____

   What would it look like? _____

   Draw your invention here.

   Personal Transportation Machine for the year 2042

Action Alphabet Class Book

Activity:

The student, small group, or class will make an alphabet book of verbs.

Materials:

- chart paper
- large pieces of construction paper (1 per child)
- stapler, hole punch and yarn, or hole punch and binding rings

- marker
- poster board
- crayons

Preparation:

1. List the alphabet letters on the chart paper, leaving space to the right of each to list words.

2. Make a front and back cover for the class book from poster board. Title ideas include "The Action Alphabet," "First Grade's Action Alphabet," and "Room 10's Action Alphabet."

Directions:

Review verbs with the children. Have the children brainstorm a list of action words, one or more per alphabet letter. Record the verbs next to the appropriate letter on the chart paper.

For a class book, allow each child to choose a letter and a corresponding verb from the list. The children will each make a page for the class book, using construction paper. Each page should contain the following:

- the alphabet letter
- the verb
- an illustration

Depending on the developmental level of the children, a sentence which includes the verb can be written on each page.

Bind the completed pages and the cover to make a book.

Recorded Story

Tape record a reading of your favorite short story. Afterwards, use headphones and listen to the story during your free time.

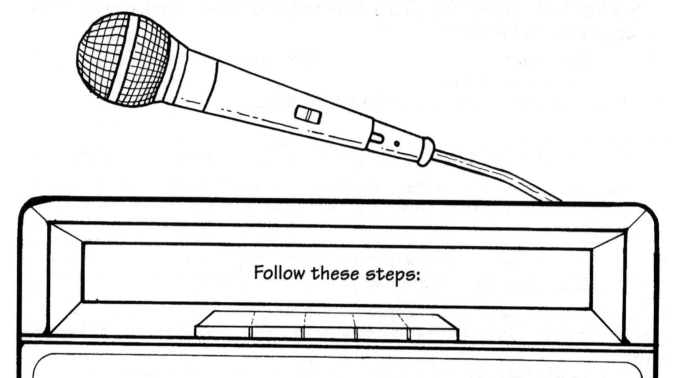

Follow these steps:

1. Choose a part of the story to read. (Your teacher may assign you a part.)

2. With a partner, practice reading with expression.

3. Sit in the order in which you will be reading your part.

4. Listen and watch as your teacher explains how to use the recorder and microphone to record your parts.

5. One at a time, you and the other readers will come up to the tape recorder and slowly read the parts you have been practicing.

6. When you have finished recording, rewind the tape. Listen to and enjoy your tape-recorded reading of the story.

Timely Chore

Each word in the time box refers to a specific time span. List the words in order from the shortest time span to the longest. Then, explain how long each time span is.

Time Span   **How Long Is It?**

1. _____

2. _____

3. _____

4. _____

5. _____

6. _____

7. _____

8. _____

9. _____

10. _____

11. _____

12. _____

Time Box

second	hour	millennium
fortnight	day	month
minute	score	century
year	decade	week

Name_____

Math Code

After reading *The Cat in the Hat* by Dr. Suess, use the Math Code to answer the riddle by solving the equations below. Then match the number and write each letter in its own answer box.

Who do you find in a big red box?

0	9	7	6	10	2	5	8	3	4
N	H	O	E	T	D	I	G	A	W

9	4	3	5	4
+1	+5	+2	−5	+4

8	6	9
−1	−6	−3

2	0	4
+1	+0	−2

8	8	4	9	9
+2	+1	+1	−9	−1

2	9	6
+8	−5	+1

Answer: Thing One and Thing Two

Cause and Effect

Name_____

Match each cause with its most likely effect.

1. _____ Bob stuck a pin in the balloon.   A. _____ We could not see a thing.

2. _____ Traci spilled her milk.   B. _____ The policeman wrote out a ticket.

3. _____ My mom drove too fast.   C. _____ We heard a big pop.

4. _____ The electricity went out.   D. _____ We were late for school.

5. _____ The alarm clock did not ring.   E. _____ There was a puddle on the floor.

Write possible causes for the following effects:

6. _____ so we left the circus early.

7. _____ so I bought a new one.

8. _____ so my mom picked us up.

9. _____ so we went to the mall.

10. _____ so I stayed in bed.

Write possible effects for the following causes:

11. My grandma was not feeling well _____

12. I did not do my homework_____

13. My brother got a yard job _____

14. My sister is too little_____

15. I do not like broccoli _____

Smelling Boxes

Objective: Students will become aware of their own sense of smell in a smelling and guessing game activity.

Materials:

- a cardboard or plastic box with lid (Old prescription bottles work well for this. Be sure they are clean and have the labels removed. Sometimes a pharmacist will donate bottles to educators.)
- a sharp object to poke or cut holes in the top of the lid
- tape to secure the lid
- cotton balls
- a variety of fragrant objects (examples: perfume, baking extracts)

Directions:

- To prepare for this activity, first create "smelling boxes." Plastic works best, providing the plastic itself does not have a very definite odor.
- Place a fragrant object or cotton ball that has been soaked in a fragrance in each box.
- During circle time or another specific time of the day, ask students to smell what is in each box and guess what the fragrance is. Let students compare their ideas. At the end of the day, reveal the contents of each box. Have students discuss what they learned from the activity.

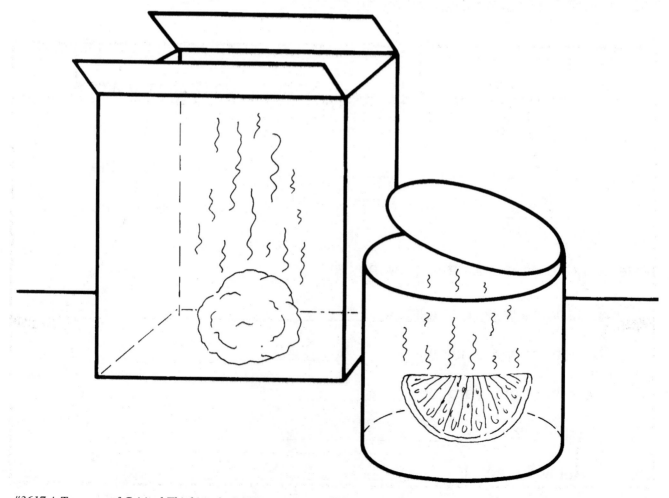

Readers' Theater

Readers' Theater is an exciting and easy method of providing students with the opportunity to perform a play while minimizing the use of props, sets, costumes, and memorization. Students read the dialogue of the announcer, narrators, and characters from prepared scripts. The dialogue may be verbatim from the book, or an elaboration may be written by the performing students. Sound effects and dramatic voices can make these much like radio plays.

In a readers' theater production, everyone in the class can be involved in some way. The twelve or more speaking parts in this readers' theater combine with the construction of signs and masks to help maximize student involvement. Encourage class members to participate in off-stage activities, such as coloring and cutting out masks, making signs to be placed around speakers' necks, serving tea and cookies, delivering invitations, and greeting guests at the door.

It is not necessary to wear costumes for a readers' theater production, but the students can wear masks, hats, or signs around their necks, indicating their speaking parts.

Prepare signs by writing a reader's character (or name of the character) on a piece of construction paper or tagboard. If possible, laminate it for durability and then, staple a necklace-length piece of yarn to the top of the paper (or punch holes and tie with yarn).

Distribute copies of the following invitation to parents and other guests.

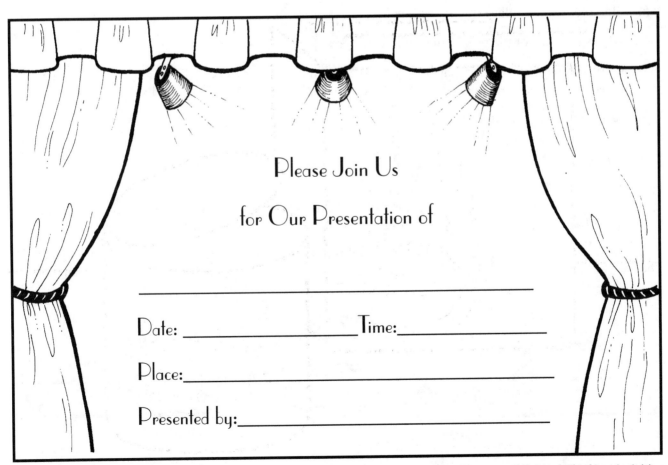

Please Join Us

for Our Presentation of

_____

Date: _____ Time:_____

Place:_____

Presented by:_____

Story Scene

A shoebox can be the center of two projects the children will enjoy.

The teacher or an older child can make samples that the primary children can copy with some assistance.

DIORAMA

Materials: a shoebox (without the lid), construction paper or shelf paper, lightweight tagboard, scissors, glue, tape, crayons or markers, magazine pictures (optional), Contac® paper to cover outside of box (optional)

Directions:

1. Cut out one side out of the shoebox.

2. Cover the outside of the box, if you wish.

3. To make a pattern for the inner walls, lay the box on the construction paper and measure the size of the three outer sides. Fold the paper around the box and cut around the outline.

4. Decorate these inner walls with drawings or magazine pictures.

5. Glue the walls in place inside the box.

6. Cover the floor of the box in the same way.

7. Tagboard and construction paper may be used to make other free-standing pictures for the scene. Consider adding other materials like foil, cotton balls, fabric, yarn, clay, and twigs (for trees).

8. Label with the title, author, and artist's name.

PARADE FLOAT

Here is where the **lid** of the shoe box comes into play. Replace the **shoebox** with its **lid**, and using the same materials as for the activity above, direct the children to make a **float** for their book. They can cover the **lid** appropriately, add free-standing forms, and even add wheels if they wish!

Either of these projects may be started in class and sent home to be completed with a parent's help. They will enjoy it while the children will have the opportunity to share their reading accomplishments.

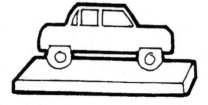

Design A Bookmark

Look at the cover of your book. Skim through and look at the pictures. See if you can design a bookmark especially for this book.

Directions:

1. Draw your ideas on the pattern below.

2. Color your drawings in bright colors.

3. Carefully cut along the solid lines.

4. Fold on the dotted line.

5. Glue the sides together.

Enjoy your reading!

BACK   **FRONT**

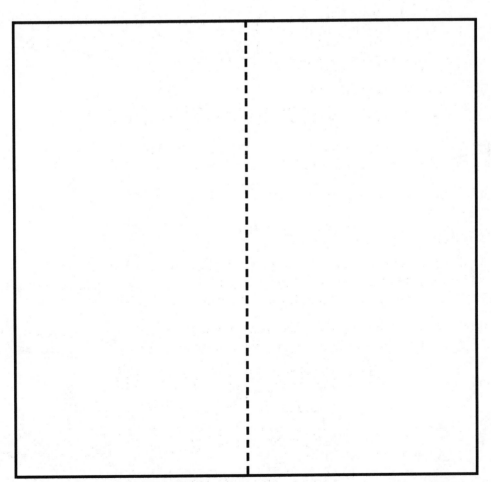

To the teacher: In place of #4 and #5 above, the two sides may be cut apart, mounted on construction paper, and the edges fringed. (See sample above.)

Ice Cream Cone Creatures

Directions: Use the cone and scoop shapes to make a creative creature. Cut out the shapes and glue them to another paper. Add any details you want with crayons and markers. Write a story about your creature.

Ice Cream Songs

Sing the following songs written to familiar tunes and then have students write others in the same way. Choose other topics to write songs about.

Take Me Out for Some Ice Cream

(sung to the tune of "Take Me Out to the Ball Game")

Take me out for some ice cream,

Take me out to the store.

Buy me a triple scoop jumbo cone.

I won't share; I will eat it alone!

So just scoop, scoop, scoop up the ice cream —

Give me three kinds I adore!

For it's one, two, three scoops to go

At the ice cream store!

Hot Fudge, Cherries, Toffee Crunch

(sung to the tune of "Twinkle, Twinkle, Little Star")

Hot fudge, cherries, toffee crunch,

Peanuts, whipped cream, lots to munch.

At the top of my ice cream,

So delicious, it's a dream!

Hot fudge, cherries, toffee crunch,

How I love to munch and munch!

Dip Deep the Silver Scoop

(sung to the tune of "Swing Low, Sweet Chariot")

Dip deep the silver scoop
Into the chocolate ice cream.
Dip deep the silver scoop
Into the chocolate ice cream.

I looked o'er the counter, and what did I see
Right by the chocolate ice cream?
Lots of hot fudge, caramel, and strawberry
To add to my chocolate ice cream.

Dip deep the silver scoop
And have some delicious ice cream.
Try a bite, or two, or three
Of this delicious ice cream.

The Ice Cream in the Bowl

(sung to the tune of "The Farmer in the Dell")

The ice cream in the bowl,
The ice cream in the bowl,
Hi-ho the dairy-o,
The ice cream in the bowl.

The ice cream takes a banana.
The ice cream takes a banana.
Hi-ho the dairy-o,
The ice cream takes a banana.

The banana takes some fudge (etc.).
The fudge takes some sprinkles (etc.).
The sprinkles take some nuts (etc.).
The nuts take some whipped cream (etc.).
The whipped cream takes a cherry (etc.).
The cherry takes a child (etc.).
The child eats the sundae (etc.).

A Poem About Me

In *The Mixed Up Chameleon* by Eric Carle, the chameleon wanted to be many things it was not. Yet being what it was not did not make it happy. It found out that being itself was best. Find out about yourself by completing the poem below.

I am _____

and _____

But I am not _____

I like _____

and _____

But I do not like _____

I am happy when _____

and _____

But I am not happy when _____

I feel good about myself when _____

and _____

But I do not feel good about myself when _____

If I could be anything, I would be _____

and _____

But, even though I could be anything, _____

I would not be _____

My Very Own Quilt

Imagine that you have been asked to design your very own quilt. The quilt should tell something about yourself, your family, your pets, or things that are special to you. What types of things would you put on your quilt?

In the space below, list some things you would like to add to your quilt. These things should "tell a story" about you. Use the Idea Bank to help you think.

Idea Bank

1. Describe your family. Do you have brothers and sisters? a mom and a dad?
2. Do you want a pet or have any pets?
3. What does your house look like? Is it one story or two?
4. Does your family have any hobbies that it does together?
5. Do you have any hobbies that you do alone?
6. Have you gone on any special trips? What do you remember the most about them?
7. Have you read any books that were special to you?
8. What is your favorite subject in school?
9. Do you have any favorite foods? Would you eat them all the time if you could?
10. Do you have a dream about your future? What do you hope to do? Tell about it.

My Ideas

_____

_____

_____

_____

_____

_____

Now, on separate paper draw a quilt picture that shows some important things from your list, things that will tell a quilt story about you.

Recipe for a Perfect Friendship

Read *Frog & Toad Together* by Arnold Lobel (HarperCollins Child Books, 1979). Toad baked some cookies for his friend Frog. Think about what it takes to make a friendship. Make up a recipe for a perfect friendship. Write it on the lines below.

── A Perfect Friendship ──

Ingredients

_____

_____

_____

_____

Directions

_____

_____

_____

_____

_____

_____

_____

_____

Bake at_____degrees for_____. Share it with a friend.

Find It

Questions

Define the word diversity. How much animal diversity is present in everyday life?

Setting the Stage

- Have students compare their ideas of what an animal is with the ideas of others in the class.
- Discuss with students various kinds of animals such as amphibians, arthropods, birds, corals, fish, jellyfish, mammals, mollusks, reptiles, sea urchins, starfish, sponges, and worms.

Materials Needed for Each Individual

- pencil and paper
- animal data chart (following page)

Procedure (Student Instructions)

1. Walk around the school yard looking for different kinds of animals.
2. On your data-capture sheet, write down the name of each animal and draw a picture of each animal that you find, including the type of animal it is. For example, a cat is a mammal and a lizard is a reptile.
3. Write two descriptive words for each animal. Each descriptive word may be used only once during the investigation.
4. Consolidate all student lists into one list on the board.
5. List animals by their types.
6. Determine which type of animal was seen most.
7. Work together as a class to come up with a list of traits all animals have in common.

Extension

Have students use a camera to take pictures of the animals to compare and classify in class.

Closure

Have students make animal journals in which to write their ideas about animals. Have each student draw a picture of his or her favorite animal seen.

Find It *(cont.)*

Complete the chart below.

Name of Animal	Type of Animal	Picture of Animal	Descriptive Words

Teaching an Alien

Think of an everyday thing you do, like washing dishes, brushing your teeth, making a sandwich, etc. Explain how to do this regular and ordinary thing to an alien who might never have even heard about the process. Be as complete and specific as you can.

This is an explanation of . . .

_____

_____

_____

_____

_____

_____

_____

_____

_____

_____

_____

_____

_____

_____

_____

_____

_____

Logs and Journals

Rationale

In order to enhance student understanding of historical events and to provide motivation for learning about events, you should read to students at least one historical picture book for each unit of study. If you feel your students are capable, then have them read an additional historical picture book on their own. With the abundant selection of wonderful historical literature available, students can be allowed to self-select the book they will read. However, if we allow students to select their own books to read, how do we keep track of their progress? Student logs and journals can be an excellent way of charting student work, progress, and attitudes for both self-selected books, and for whole class studies of particular historical literature.

Reading logs are designed to track progress and the specific amount of time spent reading. The time limit is set at your discretion. It may include the time spent during a particular unit of study. Or you may simply choose to track on a monthly basis.

A journal is one step beyond a log. In the journal, students respond to the books they are reading rather than just keeping a list of the titles. By reading your students' journals you can get a good idea of not only their reading comprehension ability but also their ability to communicate in writing. The motivation for keeping the journal is the personal response you write back to the students. When teachers and students write back and forth to each other, a more personal relationship can develop. With class sizes constantly increasing, the journal may be the only opportunity for teacher and student to have a one-to-one correspondence on a regular basis. Students will undoubtedly enjoy this special attention.

How To Use Logs and Journals

The log is simple to use. It merely requires that students record what they read during a period of time. The reading log included in this guide is for a one-month period, but you can adjust that if you wish.

Journals have a more complex purpose. After reading a story on their own, or as a class, you may ask your students to respond to the story in their journals.

"Buffalo Bill Bucks" Program

Make a copy of this list for each student to have for reference. Be generous with letting students earn money. It might also be wise to alert parents of this new system.

Give students an opportunity to spend their money as a culminating activity. Let them know the cost of an activity. For example, a special movie or story time will cost each student $500.00. Have them decide on a goal and then determine if they have enough money.

Students can earn money in these ways:

1. Each Monday, you will receive $100.00 for being in school or $20.00 a day for being in school and completing your work.
2. Any time you do outstanding class work or show good citizenship you can earn $5.00 to $20.00.
3. If the whole class has worked hard all day long, you may earn a bonus of $5.00 to $20.00.
4. Receiving 100% on classroom tests can earn from $1.00 to $20.00.
5. If you hold any type of classroom responsibility such as messenger or monitor and complete it daily, you will receive $10.00 a day.
6. If you are elected to be banker for this program and fulfill the job, you can earn $20.00.
7. Dividend payments for a Bull Market day will earn $20.00.

Students can lose money in these ways:

Breaking any class rule $10.00

Incomplete assignments (missing name, messy work) $10.00

Not following instructions $10.00

Misbehaving $15.00

Out-of-control noise $10.00

Asking if you will receive money $10.00

Tattling $5.00

Out of seat without permission (drinks, at pencil sharpener) $10.00

Bathroom privileges $5.00

Tardiness $5.00

Lost pencils replaced $10.00

Unexpected school-time problem . . . . From $1.00 to unlimited

Movement and Songs

A Tree Through the Seasons

❋ Set the mood with appropriate background music.

❋ Describe a scene so that the children can see a picture in their minds.

❋ Encourage the use of props.

❋ Suggested movements for each season:

Summer

❋ A bird is building a nest in your uppermost branches. (Pair the children. One partner is the tree swaying slowly, happily. The other partner is the bird building a nest in the other's hair. Use cotton, small twigs, and fabric scraps. Trade roles.)

Fall

❋ The wind is beginning to sway your branches. Your leaves are falling off. (Give each child a number of paper leaves or let them make their own. Have them sway and drop their leaves.)

Winter

❋ It is very cold outside now. Snow is falling on your branches. (Pair the children. One partner is the tree; arms are extended and the body is shivering. The other partner drapes snow, use white yarn or fabric on the outstretched arms. Have the children exchange roles.)

Spring

❋ Days are getting warmer now. Buds are beginning to open on your branches. (Children keep their arms at their sides as they dance joyfully. Slowly they open their hands to show the buds opening.)

A Palm Tree During a Tropical Rain Storm

❋ The rain is coming down slowly and splashing on all your branches. Now the rain is hitting you harder and harder. (Give each child a section of newspaper. Tell them to hold the paper with both hands as they wave it through the air faster and faster to make rain sounds.)

Here We Go Round the Mulberry Bush

❋ Sing and play a game of "Here We Go Round the Mulberry Bush." Music for this song can be found in *Tom Glazer's Treasury of Songs for Children* (compiled by Tom Glazer, Doubleday, 1964).

❋ Substitute other tree names for mulberry bush—Joshua tree, cypress tree, cottonwood tree, etc.

❋ Make up your own verses or use some of the following ideas.

This is how the leaves fall off, the leaves fall off, the leaves fall off.
This is how the leaves fall off, all autumn long.
(One child is the tree. The others can hold handfuls of real or paper leaves and drop them as they sing and dance around the tree.)
This is how the branches sway, branches sway, branches sway.
This is how the branches sway, all during spring.
(The children can move their arms gracefully as they sing this verse.)

Lesson Planning Activities

The following is a list of activities, projects, and materials that you can use when creating a visual/spatial lesson or when you plan to strengthen this intelligence.

- Brochures
- Collages
- Color Cues
- Color/Texture Schemes
- Designs
- Drawing
- Fantasy
- Flow Charts
- Graphic Symbols
- Guided Imagery
- Idea Sketching
- Imagination
- Labeling
- Mapping

- Mind Mapping
- Molding Clay
- Montage
- Painting
- Patterns
- Photography
- Pictures
- Picture Metaphors
- Posters
- Pretending
- Sculpting
- Texture
- Visualization

I Have a Dream

Martin Luther King Jr. had a dream that some day all people of all colors would be able to live together in peace. Tell about your dream for peace. Draw a picture to go with your story.

Musical Ideas

The following ideas and projects can easily be incorporated into a thematic unit on the environment.

Easy Listening

As a class listen to Camille Saint-Saens' *"The Carnival of the Animals"* or Igor Stravinsky's "The Rite of Spring." Have the children make up their own body movements to match the mood of the songs. Let the children paint an abstract picture after they have listened to the music. Brainstorm a list of words inspired by the music; use the list of words to write poems.

Sing a Song

Teach students the words and melody to "The Animal Fair" (A copy can be found in Tom Glazer's *Treasury of Songs for Children,* Doubleday, 1964. rev. ed. of *Treasury of Folk Songs*). Illustrate it with a class mural. Substitute forest animal or ocean animal names for the jungle animals listed in the song.

Music Makers

Make your own musical instruments (see suggestions below). Divide students into small groups. Assign each group a different topic, e.g., jungle noises, forest noises, ocean animals noises, etc. In turn, have each group perform an original composition for the class; see if the others can determine the names of the animals and/or environment.

Soft Drink Bottle Horn

Gently blow into the top of an empty soft drink bottle to produce a hollow sound.

Sandy Blocks

Wrap and tape sandpaper around two wood blocks. Gently rub them together.

Milk Carton Rattle

Clean a half-pint milk carton. Put a handful of dried peas or beans in the carton; staple shut. Shake to make rattling sound.

Coffee Can Drum

Use any size coffee can (empty) with a plastic lid. Drumsticks can be pencils, straws, fingers, brushes, etc.

Encourage the students to invent their own musical instruments and to experiment with the different sounds the instruments can make.

What's Important?

Think about something that is really important to you. It might not be important to many other people, but it is to you. Write about this important thing. What makes it important? Is it something that should be important to other people? Why or why not? (It might be a thing, or an idea, or an event—or anything else that is important to you).

_____

_____

_____

_____

_____

_____

_____

_____

_____

_____

_____

_____

_____

_____

_____

_____

_____

_____

_____

Jigsaw Task Season: Identification

Group Members   **Season**

_____   _____

_____   _____

_____   _____

_____   _____

You will be assigned to an "expert" group. In your expert group you will be given the name of a season. Your group needs to find out what the weather is like in that season and which months of the year are included in that season.

After you have learned that information in your "expert" group, you will return to your "home" group. Tell the members of your "home" group what you learned about your season.

After everyone has described his or her season, have your group make a calendar. Use the calendar below as an example. Make a label and picture for each month, naming and describing the season.

MONTH

SUNDAY	MONDAY	TUESDAY	WEDNESDAY	THURSDAY	FRIDAY	SATURDAY

Building a "Recyclable" Playground

Goal: To make children aware of recycling as a way to protect the Earth; to create a model playground using recyclable materials

Materials: Variety of recyclable materials, large cardboard carton, glue, scissors, tape, large cardboard boxes or poster board, green paint, paintbrush

Directions: Before starting the project, talk about recyclable materials. Set up a recycling center in your class. Explain that recycling is an important thing to do especially if one considers that every day so many foam cups are used that they could circle around the globe. This project can be accomplished with boxes that are labeled "Recyclable."

Discuss with children that all over the world children play in playgrounds and what type of play equipment is found there. Then, in small groups, have them brainstorm about equipment they might like to see on a playground. What would the equipment do? Would it move? How would it be made safe?

Challenge each group to use recyclable materials from the recyclable boxes and make one piece of playground equipment. Place all the equipment on a poster board or bottom of a box carton painted green. Display.

Extensions: This can be a cross-grade activity where older students work with younger students in creating a new playground.

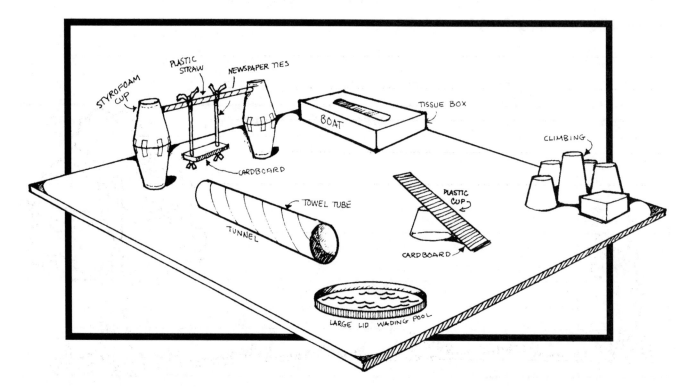

Imagine . . .

Use your imagination. Imagine that trees and flowers could speak to each other.
What would a tree have to say to a flower, and how would a flower reply?
Create a conversation between a tree and flower and write it below.

_____

_____

_____

_____

_____

_____

_____

_____

_____

_____

_____

_____

_____

_____

_____

Whose Is It?

Can you use the clues in the pictures to figure out what item belongs to each child? **Hint:** Think of the *number* of things. Write what each child owns on the line under his or her picture. Make up more puzzles like this for your classmates.

Kami owns_____ **Pablo** owns _____ **Maria** owns _____

wagon   **scooter**   **skates**

A Present for Everyone

Can you match each present to each child? **Hint:** The ones that go together have something in common. Write the present on the line under each child. Make up more puzzles like this for your classmates.

1 2 3, X Y Z

Some patterns repeat. These are patterns like 1 2 3 1 2 3 and x y z x y z. Some patterns do not repeat, but there is a connection or pattern between one thing and the next thing in a group.

For example: 1 3 5 7 9   Rule: Skip a number.

Here are some patterns using numbers and letters. Look for the rule that is used to make the patterns. Add more things to complete each pattern.

1. 2 4 6 8 10 ____ ____ ____ ____

2. AA B CC D EE ____ ____ ____ ____

3. up, cup, at, sat, it, ____, ____, ton

4. Z Y X W V U T S ____ ____ ____ ____

5. a 1 b 2 c 3 d ____ ____ ____ ____

6. December, Saturday, November, Friday, October, Thursday, September,

_____, _____, _____

7. 30 27 24 21 18 ____ ____ ____ ____

8. Amy, Barbara, Carrie, Debbie, Erin, _____ _____

9. mouse, mice, house, houses, goose, _____, _____, plants

10. 4 2 1 6 3 2 8 4 3 ____ ____ ____

Make your own patterns here. See if your friends can find the rules you used to make your patterns.

1.

2.

3.

How Many Ways?

How many ways can your group think of to divide these objects in half?

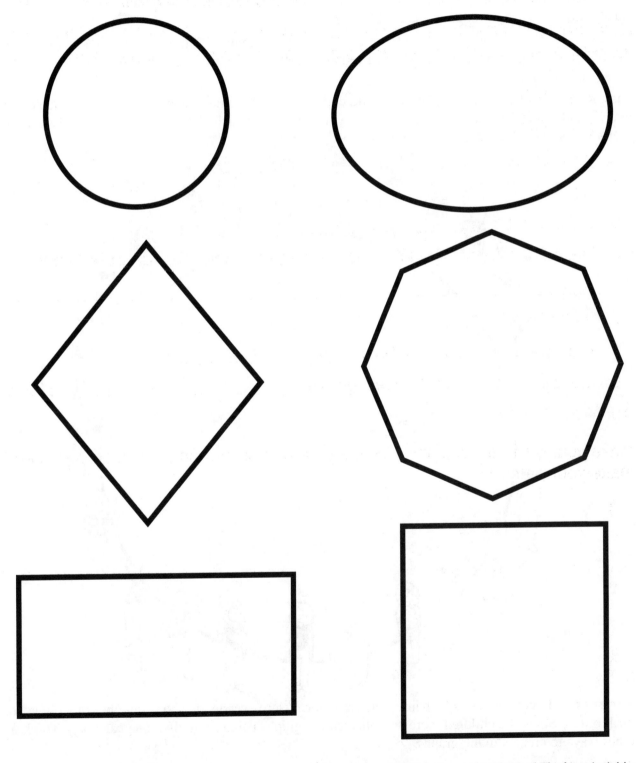

Pie Graph

Materials: chalk; paper; crayons; flat paved areas on the playground

Directions: Ask how many children are wearing the color red. Those children will need to form a line and hold hands. The children not wearing red will form a line and hold hands. The children on the ends of each line will hold hands with the children of the other group and form a large circle. One child or the teacher will draw a circle around the inside of the children with chalk. Each group will be standing together on the edge of the chalk circle.

Have the children help locate the center of the circle and place an "X" in the center. Draw lines from the "X" to the beginning and ending of the red group. Which group makes the biggest piece of the pie? This is a pie chart.

Pass out crayons and paper and let each child copy one of the human pie graphs that you made on the playground. This can be done right on the playground so that each child can remember what a pie graph looks like. Label the pie chart.

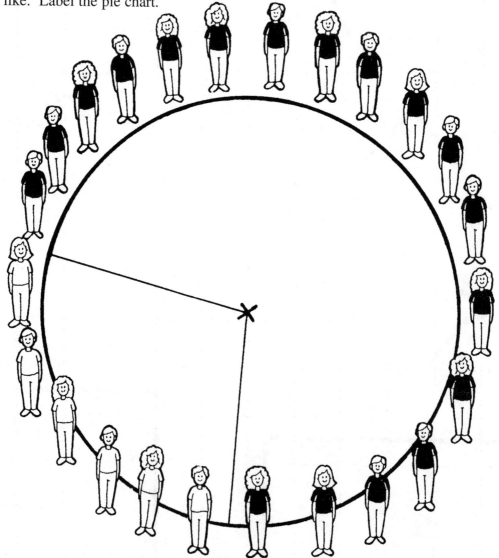

Variations: Divide the class by hair color, eye color, Velcro® versus tie shoes, number of siblings, or birth order. Show the children more complicated pie graphs using more than one category. Think of other ways to create "living graphs."

Symmetry

Look at this pattern. This is called a symmetrical pattern. That means that the pattern is balanced on all four sides. The right side is like a mirror reflection of the left. The top half is like a mirror reflection of the bottom half. Color a symmetrical pattern on the grid below. Make sure that the pattern is the same on all four sides.

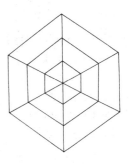

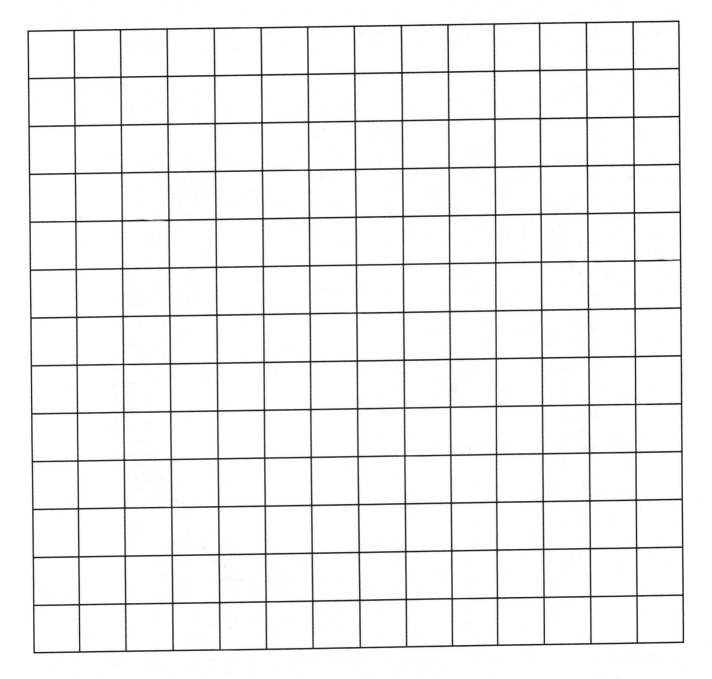

Patterns

A pattern is a group of things that repeats. Draw a line through the designs that do not repeat (the ones that are not patterns).

Look for the repeating patterns in each row and add three more things to complete the patterns.

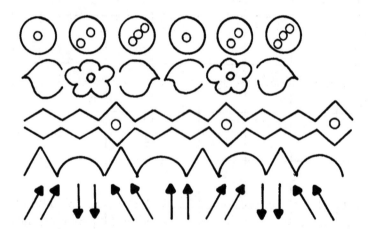

Make your own patterns below.

1.

2.

3.

4.

Accessing Logical/Mathematical Intelligence Through Musical/Rhythmic Intelligence

Background Music:

Many teachers already use background classical music during learning periods. This is a great way to help musical students feel at ease while doing something that might not come easily to them. Music that works especially well are selections that have a steady forward movement, like the "Pachelbel Canon." Extend music into the curriculum, however. Try some of the following activities.

Musical Math Facts:

Students can learn counting and other various functions of math easily when they are put to music.

Grades K–1: Fingerplays and chants that deal with counting, patterns, sequence, etc., work well to access the logical/mathematical intelligence through music and rhythm.

Grades 2–4: There are many commercially produced recordings of math facts put to music. Multiplication raps are very popular with students in the higher grades (grades 3 and 4).

Encourage students to develop their own tunes or chants for concepts with which they are having a difficult time or cooperatively develop some classwide learning tools (Interpersonal extension).

Musical Math:

Assign a different sound to various math functions. Let students perform their math problems. For instance, plus (+) might be a clap; equal (=) might be a finger snap. Doing an addition activity repetitively in this manner will help the students remember their facts. Let the students choose their own sounds for the various functions.

Musical Clues:

When students are working on solving a problem, use a selection of music to let them know, by volume signals, whether they are on target or missing the point. The closer they get to solving the problem, the louder the music gets. Use this with individual students or a whole class working on a single problem. The greater the number of students who show they have the correct answer, the louder the music becomes.

Pattern Recognition:

Students who are strong in the musical/rhythmic intelligence will have less trouble recognizing patterns in a musical context. Have them create their own patterns, using musical notes or symbols.

Estimating

Directions:

1. Choose one item and estimate (guess) how many it will take to fill one ice cream scoop.
2. Fill the scoop level with the item.
3. Count and write down the actual number in the scoop.
4. Figure out the difference between your estimate and the actual number. Write down the difference.
5. Do these steps again for another item.

Item	Estimate	Actual	Difference

Truck from Shapes

1. Tell what each shape is.
2. Cut out the shapes.

3. Put the truck together.
4. Glue the truck to another paper.

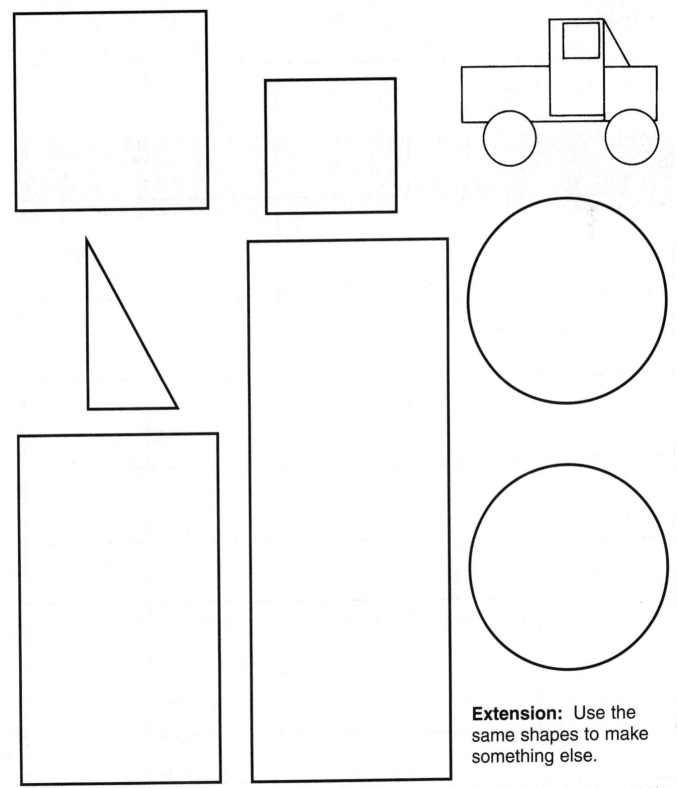

Extension: Use the same shapes to make something else.

Pattern Quilt

Quilts often use a pattern of colors and shapes to create a beautiful design. Use the grid below to make a new quilt design. A simple pattern may be made by coloring the squares (red, yellow, blue, red, green, etc.). A more complex pattern can be created by dividing the squares diagonally before coloring.

Accessing Interpersonal Intelligence Through Logical/Mathematical Intelligence

Group Problem Solving:

Any activity where students work on solving a problem or think logically in pairs, groups, or teams fits into this category. Working on math assignments together, completing a puzzle together, playing logic games together, and combining efforts on a scientific experiment are all excellent activities.

Code Clues:

Ask your students to create a code language that they can write down. Have them write a note to a classmate, using the code. A key should be included in the note. Then each recipient may respond to the note, using the same code.

This activity might be simplified by making up a class code first. Have the students write notes to each other using the class code and have the key easily visible. Once students have the hang of code writing, they might move on to develop their own codes.

Charting Individual Differences:

Have a discussion in which you point out that every person is special and different in his or her own way. Remind your students about some of the positive individual differences that are apparent in your classroom. Ask the students to interview classmates (lower grades might interview four classmates, while higher grade levels may interview as many as ten classmates).

Ask students to chart their classmates' names, hobbies, likes, and dislikes. When they are all done, you might incorporate the information into a classwide chart showing individual differences.

Math Simulations:

Students can work together in a variety of ways in this section. Younger students might play shop where they work together in figuring prices and making sure they have enough money to buy the things that they need. Older students might do the same but add complexity by using checkbooks and balancing these at the end of every month (or week). They might also work on minibudgets together.

Let students start small businesses in the classroom (in partnerships or corporations) and think of all the problems they might have to overcome. (Minisociety curriculum works very well in the third and fourth grades).

The Plant World

The study of plants requires the use of math-oriented skills. The ability to measure, compare, and graph are just a few of the skills that can bring mathematics into your plant lessons.

- Teach or review the use of measuring tools (such as rulers with centimeters and inches to measure length.)

- Have students practice reading and making charts and graphs.

- Provide opportunities for students to record data on a variety of graphs and charts. Teach the skills necessary for success.

- Encourage students to devise their own ways to show the data they have gathered.

- On an appropriate level, teach how to average test results.

- Challenge students to find mathematical connections as they study plants.

Science Concept: *The world of plants is full of recurring patterns.*

- Have students study the patterns on these cards. Have them cut the cards out and take them into nature. Can they find the same patterns in plants? How many? The use of a hand-held magnifying lens would be helpful.

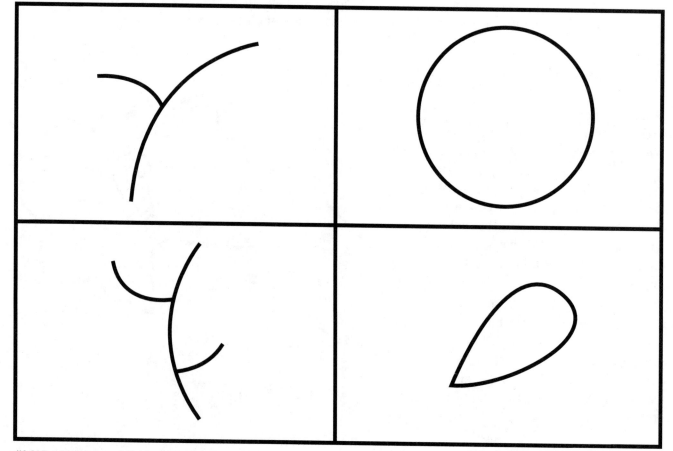

Animal Journal

Animal journals are an effective way to integrate science and language arts. Students are to record their observations, thoughts, and questions about science experiences in a journal to be kept in the science area. The observations may be recorded in sentences or sketches which keep track of changes both in the science item or in the thoughts and discussions of the students.

Animal journal entries can be completed as a team effort or an individual activity. Be sure to model the making and recording of observations several times when introducing the journals to the science area.

Use the student recordings in the animal journals as a focus for class science discussions. You should lead these discussions and guide students with probing questions, but it is usually not necessary for you to give any explanation. Students come to accurate conclusions as a result of classmates' comments and your questioning. Animal journals can also become part of the students' portfolios and overall assessment program. Journals are also valuable assessment tools for parent and student conferences.

How to Make an Animal Journal

1. Cut two pieces of 8½" x 11" (22 cm x 28 cm) construction paper to create a cover. Make a creative front cover to glue on the front of the journal.

2. Insert several animal journal pages.

3. Staple together and cover stapled edge with book tape.

Myths About Weather

Long ago when people didn't understand something, they made up an imaginary tale to explain it.

Write a myth of your own.

Imagine you lived long before there were meteorologists to help explain the weather. Now imagine that suddenly there was a terrible tornado. After it was over, all your friends and family tried to figure out what had happened and why. Put your ideas into a web. Now use your ideas to write a story.

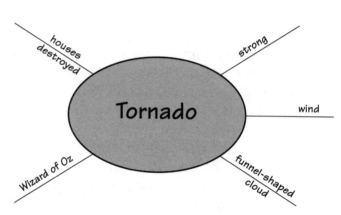

Use the blank web to collect your ideas to write a story. Make your story into a book by adding a cover. Share it with friends.

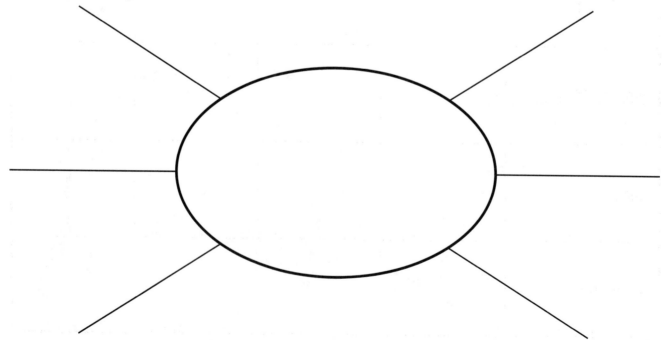

Some topics for weather myths include: lightning, hail, rainbows, hurricanes, and snow.

Animal Brain Strain

Mark an "X" in each square which is eliminated by a clue. When there is only one blank square left in a row or column within a category, put a happy face in that square.

A sloth, a spider monkey, a tree frog, and a toucan are named Fred, Harvey, Melissa, and Jana. Read the clues below to find each animal's name.

Clues:

1. Melissa is a different color than both the spider monkey and Jana.
2. The frog is younger than Fred.
3. Harvey is the oldest and is a good friend of the spider monkey.
4. Harvey and the toucan share the same tree.
5. Jana is not an amphibian.

Animal Brain Strain Chart

	Fred	Harvey	Melissa	Jana
Tree Frog				
Spider Monkey				
Sloth				
Toucan				

Plant Brain Strain

Mark an "X" in each square which is eliminated by a clue. When there is only one blank square left in a row or column within a category, put a happy face in that square.

The favorite rain forest trees and plants of David, Adam, Bianca, and Chelsey are bromeliads, orchids, ferns, and kapok trees. Read the clues below to find each person's favorite rain forest tree or plant.

Clues:

1. No person's name has the same number of letters as his or her favorite rain forest tree or plant.
2. David and the boy who likes orchids are from different tribes.
3. The kapok tree is the favorite of one of the girls.
4. Chelsey's favorite plant is a member of the pineapple family.

Chart
Plant Brain Strain

	David	Adam	Bianca	Chelsey
Bromeliad				
Orchid				
Fern				
Kapok Tree				

Physical Education

What can be more fun for primary students then imagining they are part of an ecosystem, subject to the forces that make ecosystems grow, thrive, and move? Here is an opportunity to let your students develop their knowledge of ecosystems in a physical way.

Science Concept: *the interdependence of all things in an ecosystem*

Have students stand front-to-back in a very tight circle, all facing one direction. The goal is to have everyone sit down on the knees of the person behind, without falling down. Instruct the students to sit on the count of three. Give it a try. With practice the class should be able to sit on one another's knees without the circle collapsing. Warn students to be still while sitting, as their movements will affect the rest of their classmates, just as changes in one part of the ecosystem can disrupt the entire ecosystem. Remove one of the students while the group is sitting. What happens? This is what happens when part of an ecosystem is removed.

Science Concept: *carrying capacity*

Draw a 4' x 6' (1.2 m x 1.8 m) rectangle on the playground with chalk. Tell your class that this is the ecosystem and they are the various plants and animals that live there. Have three students sit in the rectangle. Is there enough room for them? Have three more students sit in the rectangle. Is it as comfortable as it was before? Keep adding students to the rectangle until it can no longer hold anyone. How many students can the rectangle hold? This is the carrying capacity of the ecosystem. Explain to students what carrying capacity means. Ask them what factors, besides size, may affect the carrying capacity of an ecosystem (food and water availability).

Assessment Strategies

Science Artwork

Young children love to draw. "Pictures speak a thousand words." It is appropriate, and acceptable, to utilize children's artwork as a means of assessment. An excellent year-long science artwork assessment tool is a Science Art Journal which will contain artwork from all topics learned during science time.

To make an artwork journal, begin by punching three holes on the short left side of two 12" x 18" (30 cm x 45 cm) pieces of tagboard and ten to fifteen sheets of cut 12" x 18" (30 cm x 45 cm) chart/butcher paper. Create a book by sandwiching the chart/butcher sheets between the tagboard cover sheets. Line up the left short side and punch three holes (top, middle, bottom) through the entire thickness. Thread a short piece of string through each hole and tie in a knot or bow (make certain that the pages can turn easily before knotting tightly), or alternatively, open three small metal clasp rings and place through the three holes and shut rings. Write "The 'Art' of Science" and the child's name on the cover. When the child has completed the first piece of artwork you want to place in the journal, simply glue or tape the artwork to the first sheet of chart/butcher paper. Then place the date in the top corner and write any comments you and/or the child desires to make pertaining to the piece of artwork.

This is an excellent tool to use during parent-teacher conferences. It is also a great resource for the child's next teacher. This type of visual log can follow the growth that took place during a number of years if the continuing teacher simply adds more pages to the back of the book.

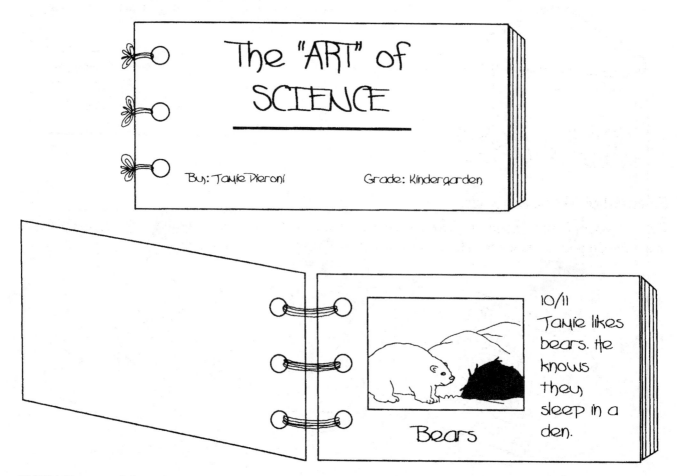

Assessment Strategies *(cont.)*

Science Projects

Provide opportunities throughout the year for children to create projects based on their science topics or themes. Among the most popular for the young learner are these:

Posters   **Dioramas**

Mobiles   **Student-Created Bulletin Boards**

Scientist at Work (Photographs)

Keep a camera in the classroom and regularly take pictures of "learning in progress." Keep the pictures in a photographic time line to refer to during assessment and evaluation processing.

A Magnetic Masterpiece

Science Concept: Magnets can be used doing everyday tasks.

Have children try using magnets to paint.

1. Put a few objects made of iron or steel in some tempera paint.
2. Have children cut a piece of white paper to fit the bottom of a shallow glass baking dish.
3. Tell children to put the paper in the bottom of the glass dish.
4. Have children put the paint-coated objects into the dish.
5. Have each child takes a turn being a magnet artist and move a magnet under the dish to pull the paint-coated iron and steel objects around on the paper to make a painting.

Create an Environmental Flyer

Directions: Select a topic or problem such as the greenhouse effect, air pollution, acid rain, hazardous waste, etc. Use that topic or problem as the basis of a flyer to create awareness and generate solutions for your community.

Topic or Problem to Identify

_____

_____

_____

_____

Solutions to Suggest

_____

_____

_____

_____

Draw a draft of your flyer here and then draw it on art paper. If possible, duplicate the flyers and distribute them in your community (but do not create waste).

Animal Sounds

Singing songs about animals, selecting orchestral numbers to "promote" the importance of animals and making animal sounds in groups are just a few of the ways to integrate music into your animal-based lessons.

Science Concept: *Animals make sounds for many reasons*

- Have you ever been outside at night when all you can hear are the animals? Almost everyone has heard crickets and howling dogs. Animals can make such interesting sounds. Each is like a musical instrument.

- Create your own classroom symphony orchestra of animals. Decide which animal sounds you want in the orchestra. Assign students to make those sounds. You can have a symphony depicting the sounds of any type of animal environment you like. For example, the desert, the forest, or the rain forest can be depicted by your animal symphony.

- "Animals" making the same sounds should be in the same group. Let the students take turns conducting the orchestra. They can make any kind of rhythm they want.

Perfect Pitch

Background

If we talk about making a high sound, are we referring to pitch or volume? (pitch) The concept of pitch is something that many young children do not understand. Even if they understand that there are different musical notes, they have trouble identifying which ones are higher in pitch. This experiment gives them the opportunity to explore what pitch is.

Objectives

- to understand the concept of pitch
- to make and then test predictions

Student Instruction

Explain the difference between volume and pitch. Demonstrate higher and lower volumes, using louder and softer sounds and then demonstrate different pitches. This could be done with a musical instrument such as a piano or recorder, by singing different notes, or by using examples from the animal kingdom. For example, a mouse makes a high-pitched squeak while a lion has a low-pitched roar. Point out that these two animals also have different volumes because a lion's roar is louder than a mouse's squeak.

If you are going to have students fill the bottles themselves, introduce the funnel, what it is used for, and how to use it.

Center Preparation

Materials: 3 identical glass bottles, 12-16 ounce (360-500 mL) size; 1 metal teaspoon (5 mL); water; pitcher; 1 funnel; a 12" (30 cm) ruler; bath towel

Directions: Cover the table in the center with a bath towel. This helps absorb the spills and keeps the glass bottles from slipping off the table. Provide a metal teaspoon and three identical bottles from juice or soft drinks with lids. Label them *A*, *B*, and *C*. Pour water into each bottle, making sure there are different amounts in each. For younger students, fill the bottles ahead of time, and put on the lids to minimize spills. If you are going to have students fill the bottles, you will need a funnel and an easy-to-use pitcher.

Follow-Up Activities

Have students predict how the size and shape of a bottle will affect its pitch. Get several bottles and jars of different sizes, and allow students to try them out. Note that there are many variables in this follow-up experiment, so the results are likely to be different from what you would expect. In other words, this is not a controlled experiment. However, this type of follow-up still helps reinforce the basic concepts and motivates students toward doing their own explorations.

Relate the partially filled bottles to a flute, recorder, or clarinet. As you close more of the holes on these instruments, you effectively make the air column longer. This is analogous to taking water out of the bottles to achieve a lower pitch.

Make a Violin and Bow

Use the following directions to make a violin and bow.

Materials:

- empty tissue box
- 5 wide rubber bands
- rubber bands of different widths
- pencil, unsharpened

Directions:

1. Place a rubber band on your pencil by stretching it from the eraser to the other end.

2. Place four rubber bands on the tissue box over the opening. Be sure they are about $^1/_2$ inch (1.25 cm) apart from one another.

3. Rub your bow (the pencil with the rubber band) across your violin (the tissue box with the rubber bands).

Now try using rubber bands of different widths. How does the width of the rubber bands change the sound they make?

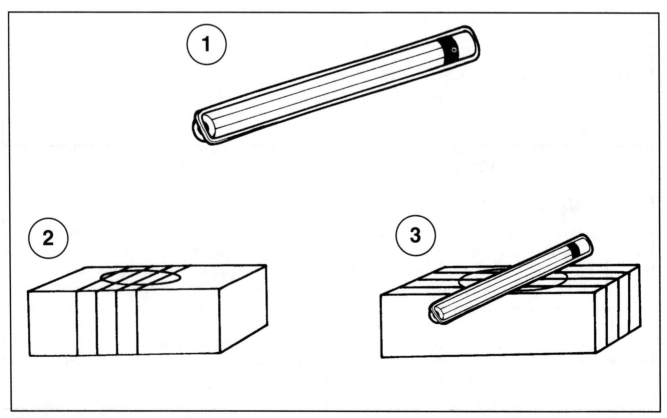

Rain Forest Dictionary

Make your own rain forest dictionary. Cut out the boxes. In each box write what the word means.
Draw a picture. Put the pages in ABC order. Staple the pages together with the cover on top.

My Rain Forest Dictionary by_____	**equator**
rain forest	**understory**
canopy	**layers**

Communications

Question

Why is it important to communicate accurately?

Setting the Stage

- Have students play the communications game "Telegraph." Whisper a message into someone's ear, and have him or her whisper the message into someone else's ear. The message may only be spoken once and not repeated. Continue telegraphing the message in whispers. Have the last person tell the class what the message was.
- Discuss with students the importance of making sure that what you say is understood.

Materials Needed for Each Group

- two sets of space shapes (page 159), one per student
- scissors

Note to the teacher: The children will work in pairs.

Procedure (Student Instructions)

1. Each pair will sit back-to-back so that they cannot see their partner's desk.
2. The Senders will arrange the shapes on their desks in any configuration desired. They will then communicate to the Receivers where each shape is located and the orientation of the shape.
3. The Receivers will arrange the shapes on their desks in the positions that they think correspond to the messages being received. The Receivers may not ask questions!
4. After all of the information has been sent and received, compare the two arrangements of figures.
5. Take turns being Senders and Receivers.

Extensions

- Have students repeat the experience allowing the Receivers to ask questions. Which method works best?
- Have students use the same process, only this time the Senders have drawn a simple picture and need to transmit the picture without saying what the picture is. They will only describe how to draw it. The Receivers will attempt to draw the same picture.

Closure

Have students compare experiences from each group. Ask them what kinds of directions produced the best results? Discuss applications to flight controllers. How Do Machines "Think" and Communicate?

The Big Why

This activity will point out the difficulty in communicating exact instructions. One method that works well is to use the hours of the clock as a reference for directions. Older children might use a coordinate grid method. The children were working on a flat desk —two dimensions. Imagine the problems involved when you are in an airplane and have to deal in three dimensions!

Communications *(cont.)*

Cut out shapes before beginning the activity.

For the Love of Animals

Create a mini-zoo by adopting a class pet. Below is information on taking care of the three most common classroom pets.

Goldfish

- 2-3 common or fantail goldfish
- large goldfish bowl
- aquarium gravel
- water (Make certain it is pure.)
- commercial fish food
- fish net

1. Place aquarium gravel in bottom of fishbowl approximately 1" (2.5 cm) thick.
2. Pour pure water (no chlorine) into fishbowl until 2" (5 cm) from rim.
3. Place purchased fish, still in purchased plastic bag of water, inside the bowl. (Bag will float near top.) Let float for 15 minutes, allowing the goldfish to become acclimated to water temperature in the fishbowl. Using a net, transfer the goldfish from bag to bowl. Feed fish a pinch of food once a day.
4. Change water once a week. (If fish are coming to the surface to breathe with mouths, change water immediately.) Pour small amount of current fish water into a plastic bag; add fish to bag with net; change water in bowl, including rinsing out gravel; then follow Step 3.

Gerbils

- two male or two female gerbils
- water bottle
- shallow, heavy dish for food
- exercise wheel
- gerbil litter
- commercial gerbil food*
- glass or plastic cage (An old aquarium with wire mesh "roof" works well.)
- hiding places (e.g., old baby shoe, empty tin can, etc.)

1. Line bottom of cage with thick layer of gerbil litter.
2. Place eating dish and drinking bottle in easy reach of gerbils' mouths.
3. Place exercise wheel and hiding place(s) in corners of cage.
4. Place gerbils in cage. Secure wire mesh or lid of cage well. (Gerbils like to get out.) Make sure gerbils always have water. Feed gerbils at the same time each day.
5. Change gerbil litter once a week, wiping out bottom of cage before adding fresh gerbil litter.

    * Gerbils also like fresh carrots, sunflower seeds, lettuce, cabbage, apples, peas, and a little grass.

Rabbit

- newspaper
- hiding place (shoe box with opening)
- two heavy bowls (for food and water)
- rabbit and rabbit hutch (wire cage on wooden frame so cage is elevated off ground)
- commercial dry rabbit pellet food, piece of wood (for rabbit to gnaw on), fresh raw vegetables

1. Lay down newspaper (keep folded). Place frame on top of paper and cage on top of frame.
2. Place water/dry food in heavy bowls; put inside cage. Add hiding place and wood for gnawing.
3. Put rabbit in cage and secure door. Make certain rabbit always has water and dry pellets. Give fresh vegetables (favorites: carrots, lettuce, and dandelion greens) daily, but always take out leftovers at night. Change newspaper daily, too.